PREGNANT AT WORK

ANTHROPOLOGIES OF AMERICAN MEDICINE:
CULTURE, POWER, AND PRACTICE
General Editors: Paul Brodwin, Michele Rivkin-Fish, and Susan Shaw

Transnational Reproduction: Race, Kinship, and Commercial Surrogacy in India
Daisy Deomampo

Unequal Coverage: The Experience of Health Care Reform in the United States
Edited by Jessica M. Mulligan and Heide Castañeda

The New American Servitude: Political Belonging among African Immigrant Home Care Workers
Cati Coe

War and Health: The Medical Consequences of the Wars in Iraq and Afghanistan
Edited by Catherine Lutz and Andrea Mazzarino

Inequalities of Aging: Paradoxes of Independence in American Home Care
Elana D. Buch

Reproductive Injustice: Racism, Pregnancy, and Premature Birth
Dána-Ain Davis

Living on the Spectrum: Autism and Youth in Community
Elizabeth Fein

Adverse Events: Race, Inequality, and the Testing of New Pharmaceuticals
Jill A. Fisher

Motherhood on Ice: The Mating Gap and Why Women Freeze Their Eggs
Marcia C. Inhorn

Violence Never Heals: The Lifelong Effects of Intimate Partner Violence for Immigrant Women
Allison Bloom

Conceiving Christian America: Embryo Adoption and Reproductive Politics
Risa Cromer

Pregnant at Work: Low-Wage Workers, Power, and Temporal Injustice
Elise Andaya

Pregnant at Work

Low-Wage Workers, Power, and Temporal Injustice

Elise Andaya

NEW YORK UNIVERSITY PRESS

New York

NEW YORK UNIVERSITY PRESS
New York
www.nyupress.org

© 2024 by New York University
All rights reserved

Library of Congress Cataloging-in-Publication Data
Names: Andaya, Elise, 1976– author.
Title: Pregnant at work : low-wage workers, power, and temporal injustice / Elise Andaya.
Description: New York, NY : New York University Press, [2023] |
Series: Anthropologies of American medicine: culture, power, and practice |
Includes bibliographical references and index.
Identifiers: LCCN 2023017299 | ISBN 9781479817580 (hardback ; alk. paper) | ISBN 9781479817597 (paperback ; alk. paper) | ISBN 9781479817603 (ebook) | ISBN 9781479817610 (ebook other)
Subjects: LCSH: Pregnant women—Employment—New York (State)—New York. | Prenatal care—New York (State)—New York. | Working poor—Medical care—New York (State)—New York.
Classification: LCC HD6055.2.U62 N493 2023 | DDC 331.4/4—dc23/eng/20230512
LC record available at https://lccn.loc.gov/2023017299

This book is printed on acid-free paper, and its binding materials are chosen for strength and durability. We strive to use environmentally responsible suppliers and materials to the greatest extent possible in publishing our books.

Manufactured in the United States of America

10 9 8 7 6 5 4 3 2 1

Also available as an ebook

For my husband, Lindsey, with so much love and gratitude for all the time we have shared

CONTENTS

Introduction: Time and the Reproduction of Inequality in the Low-Wage Service Sector — 1

1. Service Labor and Temporal Governance in the "City That Never Sleeps" — 33

2. Working While Pregnant: Conflicts between Labor, Clinical, and Gestational Time — 65

3. Clinical Time and Racialized Inequality in Safety Net Prenatal Care — 95

4. Cosmologies of Care: Temporal Justice and the Politics of Value — 119

Epilogue: Time to Care — 149

Acknowledgments — 165

Notes — 171

Bibliography — 173

Index — 187

About the Author — 197

Introduction

Time and the Reproduction of Inequality in the Low-Wage Service Sector

It's another busy day on the women's health floor at Beaumont Hospital, a public safety net hospital in New York City.[1] The four clinical suites that annually provide gynecological, prenatal, and postpartum care to thousands of people are filled with patients awaiting their appointments. Many are heavily pregnant, with a partner, family member, or small child in tow. A few spill out of the suite into the plastic chairs lining the hallway, while others line up outside various offices to see the financial counselor, the nutritionist, or the cashier.

At this particular moment, Mary-Ann Joseph and I are wedged into uncomfortable wooden school chairs in the dimly lit classroom that hospital administrators have kindly made available to me for interviews. It's not ideal. The chairs have permanently fixed writing tables that force even me, with my non-pregnant body, to twist uncomfortably to slip into the seat, while the women whom I interview must sit at an odd sideways angle to accommodate their pregnant bellies. Yet the room does offer some valuable privacy, since the windows opening on to the hallway are blocked by shelves crammed with handouts about breastfeeding and infant sleeping practices. Most of this literature is offered in Haitian Creole and in English, reflecting the composition of the surrounding Black-majority neighborhoods where many patients have long-standing ties to the French- or English-speaking Caribbean islands. Against other windows, decades-old stacks of yellowing pamphlets on HIV—a reminder of an earlier time in New York City's history—shield us from the constantly passing patients and hospital staff and provide a measure of confidentiality not possible elsewhere in the clinic.

Mary-Ann is a tall, soft-spoken woman with a gentle, worried air, originally from the small Caribbean island of Saint Vincent. Now thirty-nine years old and pregnant with her fifth child, she works in the clothing section of a large department store. It's never easy, but it's even harder now; the job entails hours on her feet, bending and picking up discarded garments from the fitting rooms or the shop floor, or moving heavy boxes of clothes from storage to the front of the store. As a part-time employee, she is often scheduled for as few as fifteen hours each week. Ten dollars an hour, even when combined with her husband's income, is still a paltry sum with which to support themselves and their two young children, let alone contribute to the upkeep of her two adolescents, who had remained in Saint Vincent with her ex-husband. Sometimes, she tells me, she has so few hours that it is hardly worth the hour-and-a-half subway commute it often takes her to reach the store from her home. Whenever she can, she supplements her income by working at a senior care center closer to home, although her constantly shifting hours at the retail store make scheduling at her second job difficult.

Now midway through her second trimester of pregnancy, Mary-Ann has been able to attend most of her prenatal appointments. But with the experience of four previous pregnancies behind her, she is already dreading her last month, when she will be expected to attend prenatal care every week. Her schedule at the department store is unpredictable: shifts are posted on Sundays for the upcoming week, meaning that at times she has fewer than twenty-four hours' notice before she has to present herself at work. The discovery that she has been assigned to an early Monday morning shift necessitates a flurry of phone calls on Sunday afternoon to locate a trusted neighbor who can take her two young children to school after her husband leaves for his own job. "It's exhausting," she confides. "It's like they don't even care that we have lives as well."

Adding prenatal care to this already difficult balance means one more scheduling headache. She is always anxious about the weeks when she has a prenatal appointment, checking her work schedule as soon as it is posted and hoping that her work and prenatal responsibilities do not conflict. If they do, she has to move quickly to advertise her shift on the store's online system, although she gets so few hours that it pains her to give up any. There is also always the risk that no one will pick up the shift, especially if it is at a particularly undesirable time. In that case, she must choose between delaying her prenatal appointment and missing her work shift, thereby incurring a loss of income and a black mark on her work record. Although technically her right to paid time off to attend prenatal care is protected by New York City's Pregnant Workers Fairness Act and the Earned Sick Time Act (also known as the Paid Sick Leave Law), both of which went into effect in 2014, Mary-Ann had never heard of these protections.[2] When I tell her about them, she is doubtful that they could be of help to her. She's seen too many pregnant co-workers pushed out of their jobs for reasons that supposedly had nothing to do with their pregnancy.

Mary-Ann's anxiety is heightened by her supervisor's unsympathetic attitude toward the physical discomforts of pregnancy. It is hard to be on her feet for hours with only a couple of ten-minute breaks in between. Toward the end of a long shift, her feet swell uncomfortably in her work shoes and, now that her belly is protruding more, her lower back aches constantly from all the bending and lifting. She had asked to be assigned to duties, such as cashiering, that would allow her to sit for some period of her shift, but her supervisor—"a mother herself!" Mary-Ann exclaimed—simply responded, "If you can't do the job, then you can't do *this* job." Given this barely veiled threat, it was hard to imagine that she would be open to scheduling Mary-Ann's work shifts around more frequent prenatal care requirements. For now, Mary-Ann was trying to make it to all her prenatal appointments, despite her frustration at the frequently long waits at Beaumont Hospital. Sighing deeply, she observed, "Look at me now. I came at one [o'clock in the afternoon]. It's now four and I'm still here waiting. They don't respect my time."

These struggles over time are the focus of this book, which traces pregnant low-wage service workers' efforts to navigate the disjunctive temporal structures of service sector labor and safety net prenatal care. It shows how service workers' experiences of pregnancy and access to routine prenatal care are fundamentally shaped by these disparate *temporal regimes*, understood as the repetitive structures of time produced as "humans negotiate their temporally situated power relations with each other via discourses, histories, cultures, bodies, and technologies" (Bjork and Buhre 2021, 178; Torres 2021). Central to this book's analysis is the concept of *temporal governance*, which I define as the practices and policies of social institutions, from cities and nation-states to healthcare facilities and corporations, that produce, regulate, and enforce specific structures of time. Temporal governance is concretized in such forms as state labor regulations, workplace policy about lateness or absences, or institutional guidelines about scheduling patients, yet its local effects ultimately depend on a constellation of other factors, including the practices of individuals who decide when to abide by formal regulations and when to ignore them (and for whom). State and corporate policy, for example, might mandate that workers be given a rest break after a certain period of time on the clock. Employees in some workplaces, however, might regularly be asked to work through their break to resolve workflow issues produced by unexpected customer demand or inadequate staffing. Similarly, in clinical settings, policies around scheduling and attending patients aim to produce a regular tempo of care. In practice, provider delays, technological hiccups, and patient complications cause constant and predictable deviation from this ideal. This constant interplay between formal policy and actual practice produces the site-specific temporal regimes in which people must operate.

At its broadest level, this book is concerned with how inequalities of gender, race, class, and immigration status, among others, are reproduced through the governance of time. A robust social scientific literature has interrogated the relationship between time and power, revealing how the social organization of time reflects and reproduces broader social hierarchies (e.g., Bear 2016; Clawson and Gerstel 2014; Fabian 1983; Greenhouse 1996; Jacobs and Gerson 2004; Munn 1992; Schwartz 1974;

Thompson 1967; Zerubavel 1979). Of particular interest have been the deeply stratified hierarchies of life and labor under capitalist modalities; in the biopolitics of (neoliberal) capitalist temporal regimes, the time of some institutions, social groups, or individuals (that of corporations or CEOs, for example) is considered valuable, and is optimized through policies and practices designed to streamline productivity, enhance profit, and ensure that none of their precious time is "wasted." By contrast, the time of individuals and collectivities with less status and fewer resources is devalued, considered important only insofar as it supports the needs of more powerful people and processes. Those people lower on this socio-temporal hierarchy must reshape the rhythms of their own lives to accommodate these demands or make themselves vulnerable to economic and social marginalization (e.g., A. Cooper 2015; Harms 2013; O'Neill 2017; Sharma 2014; Snyder 2016).

Through a focus on pregnancy and access to prenatal care, this book engages with a growing scholarly and policy conversation pressing for greater attention to the temporal structures that shape the conditions of life and labor for different groups of people, exposing some to risk and harm (e.g., Boushey 2016; Clawson and Gerstel 2014; Henly and Lambert 2014; Odell 2023; O'Neill 2017; Sharma 2014; Snyder 2016; Torres 2021; Williams 2006). Centering reproduction within this analysis of time and inequality draws attention to what I call *reproductive temporalities*, by which I mean the temporal structures that unevenly shape reproductive experiences and outcomes at the level of both individuals and populations. The reproductive temporalities produced through service work, for example, are inextricable from a deeply racialized and classed social organization of time; the biological and social reproduction of wealthier families and social groups is accomplished in large part by the (re)structuring of the time of other families and social groups to make them available to work at the times that their services are desired (Sharma 2014). Yet, as Mary-Ann's narrative underscores, the time of service workers is devalued both in the workplace and in the safety net health institutions where they may expend hours waiting for care. The intersection of these and other temporal regimes in turn produces the structures of time that shape workers' experiences of reproducing children and households.

Time is thus invisibly central to processes and practices of stratified reproduction, a term coined by Shellee Colen (1995) to describe how the reproductive capacity of some groups is ideologically valued and politically enabled while that of others is discouraged and devalued. In highlighting the role of time in the reproduction of inequality, I build on the insights of anthropologists and other social scientists who have conceptualized power not as the simple oppression of one group by another (employers over employees, for example, or the state over its low-income citizens) but as the "network of practices, institutions, and technologies that sustain positions of domination and subordination in a particular domain" (Bordo 1997, 2). The constant temporal conflicts that structure the reproductive temporalities of Mary-Ann's life, as well as her limited power to reconcile them, are neither inevitable nor the product of a single vector of domination. Viewing her experiences through a diagnostic of power reveals the interlocking hierarchies of race, class, gender, and nationality, among others, that determine our varied and uneven resources to "plan a life" (Bear 2016, 489).

The voices of Mary-Ann and others in this book thus reveal how the lesser social value assigned to certain classed, raced, and gendered persons is produced and reiterated through temporal regimes and forms of temporal governance that devalue their time. In so doing, they also powerfully articulate how social hierarchies are made *real* to people through the embodied and affective sensations of frustration, stress, and boredom that arise as they endure temporal structures not of their making (Auyero 2012; O'Neill 2017). In the uneven effects of temporal governance and the life experiences that it engenders, social inequality is (re)produced in and through pregnant bodies, social institutions, and across the generations.

Race, Class, and Gender in Service Sector Labor: A Brief Overview

Service work is not by any means a new phenomenon; in the United States, low-income people and people of color have long histories of both coerced and "voluntary" labor as household and domestic help in the service of wealthier households. Yet the importance of the service sector in the US economy has grown exponentially, driven by shifting domestic and international political-economic and ideological agendas (Boris and Parreñas 2010; Kalleberg 2009, 2018). In macroeconomic theory, the service (or tertiary) sector is defined as the part of the economy that provides services, as opposed to the extraction of raw materials (the primary sector) or the manufacturing of goods (the secondary sector). In 1919 the service sector accounted for less than half of the Gross Domestic Product (GDP) of the United States. By 2019, it generated an estimated 85 percent of the country's GDP and employed four out of five Americans in the private sector (Barnes, Bauer, and Edelberg 2022; CFI 2021). The service sector's dramatic increase as a share of the economy has been fueled, on the one hand, by the late twentieth-century expansion of the knowledge industries and government services that employ so-called "white-collar" workers and, on the other, by the decline in American manufacturing that forced "blue-collar" workers into the rapidly growing low-wage service industries. The twenty-first-century service economy thus encompasses high-status and often extremely well-remunerated professional positions in areas such as corporate law and global finance as well as the platform of low-wage and low-status jobs that service them (Ehrenreich and Hochschild 2003; Sassen 1999). Despite this variation, I use the term "service sector" in this book to refer to the latter group of workers, who earn minimum or near-minimum wage in frequently unstable jobs with few opportunities for significant upward mobility.

In the mid-twentieth century, manufacturing provided a large swathe of the male labor force, particularly white workers, with stable, relatively well-paying, and sometimes unionized jobs. Male wages from industrial employment thus formed the economic basis for the enactment of a particular middle-class (white) domesticity represented by a male breadwinner and a domestic wife. By the 1970s, international competition had put increasing pressure on this sector. Over the next decades, deregulation and automation drained the power of unions and undermined social protections and minimum wage legislation, allowing companies to cut costs by restructuring their workforce to include a greater proportion of part-time, temporary, and contract labor. In what has been termed the Great Risk Shift (Hacker 2006), corporations began to off-load economic risk onto an underemployed and unpredictably scheduled workforce rather than assuming financial responsibility for supporting full-time employees.

During this same period, global financial institutions such as the International Monetary Fund (IMF) and the World Bank vigorously promoted neoliberal policies of structural adjustment in the Global South. As one facet of these new economic priorities, they made loans to "developing" countries conditional on their agreement to "open up" to foreign companies by eliminating many financial and social protections. Lured by the promise of lower labor costs, fewer taxes, and less regulatory oversight, US manufacturers decamped to countries such as Mexico, China, and Indonesia where wages were low and labor and environmental protections were weak. In 2016 the number of people employed in steelworking, one of America's traditional manufacturing sectors, had dropped to just sixty-four thousand people nationwide (Appelbaum 2016). By contrast, jobs in the care economy, such as home health care, accounted for 74 percent of job growth in the lowest fifth of the wage structure, making it one of the strongest and fastest-growing hiring sectors, particularly for women (Winant 2021). While families of color had always depended more heavily on women's paid labor given racist employment practices that discriminated against male workers of color, the decline of American manufacturing fundamentally destabilized cultural models of a breadwinner husband and a non-wage-earning wife. Between the 1950s and the 1990s, female participation in the paid labor force steadily climbed, driven variously by economic necessity and the desire for new forms of gendered self-actualization through paid work. Notably, female labor participation has stalled and even dropped since the 1990s, due largely to the scarcity of affordable and high-quality childcare options and, more recently, to the COVID-19 pandemic and its disproportionate impact on working women (Smialek 2021; Toossi 2002).

These large-scale social and economic shifts have brought about an explosive growth in inequality, as well as "a dualized organization of social reproduction, commodified for those who can pay for it, privatized for those who cannot—all glossed by the even more modern ideal of the 'two-earner family'" (Fraser 2016, 104). The dismantling of the factory-based family wage integrated women into a service economy that was deeply stratified along race, class, and gender lines (Massengill 2013). In middle-class families, women's participation in paid employment constricted their time for care work, defined as the "multifaceted labor that produces the daily living conditions that make basic human health and well-being possible" (Zimmerman, Litt, and Bose 2006, 3), still obstinately feminized and located within the "private" domestic sphere. Yet at the same time, their incorporation into higher-paid professional occupations also meant the influx of money that could be directed toward the outsourcing of reproductive labor. Tasks that been the province of the unpaid housewife, such as household chores, food provisioning and preparation, childcare, and eldercare, increasingly shifted into a low-wage labor sector comprised disproportionately of low-income women of color (Boris and Parreñas 2010; Ehrenreich and Hochschild 2003).

In working-class families, the virtual disappearance of traditionally masculine living-wage jobs made female wages, largely earned in the service sector, an indispensable part of the household income. Positions in retail, food preparation, hospitality, domestic work, and home health care surged in response to both deindustrialization and the increased demand for service labor, becoming the primary employment options for (female) workers with few educational qualifications (Winant 2021). For low-income women of color, this was largely a continuation of the same types of labor in which they had long been engaged (Glenn 1992). The 1996 "welfare-to-work" amendments passed by the Clinton administration, which capped welfare entitlements under the guise of promoting personal responsibility and incentivizing work, also forced hundreds of thousands of impoverished mothers into the low-wage workforce (Hildebrandt and Stevens 2009). There they were joined by growing numbers of female migrants from the Global South, which Saskia Sassen (1999) has called the "lower circuits of globalization," fleeing countries destabilized by structural adjustment policies, colonial legacies, and violence. In a further example of stratified reproduction, these female migrants often left, or were forced to leave, their own children in the care of others in their home countries while they cared for wealthier families and households abroad (Colen 1995; Ehrenreich and Hochschild 2003; Hondagneu-Sotelo and Avila 1997; Parreñas 2005).

Yet women's employment in poorly remunerated and low-status service jobs could not offset the overall loss of household income during this period. Between 1979 and 2012, while the wealth of the country's highest earners increased dramatically, income for the lowest third of households actually fell by 2.4 percent, due in large part to the low wages offered by service sector employers (Boushey 2016). Today, low-wage workers, defined as those earning less than two-thirds of the median hourly wage, make up a greater share of the workforce in the United States than in any of the other thirty-seven countries in the international Organization for Economic Cooperation and Development (Desmond 2023).

These intersecting geopolitical, economic, and social processes thus produced a vulnerable female labor force that could be tapped for America's growing demand for service and care work. Since the Great Recession of 2008, one-third of women's net job gains have been in low-wage positions, almost entirely in the service sector, a trend that has been predicted to continue over the next decades (Business Insider

2019; National Women's Law Center 2014). Women make up more than half of the 53 million low-wage workers in the United States, with Black and Latinx women most likely to be employed in poorly remunerated service positions (Ross and Bateman 2019). Although the face-to-face racial hierarchy of earlier domestic service has largely been exchanged for the more impersonal structural hierarchy of service work, Black and brown women continue to occupy the lowest rungs of the occupational ladder, denied opportunities for upward mobility through the interlocking oppressions of racism, sexism, and poverty (Glenn 1992). Many of the women whom I interviewed expressed the hope that service work would lead to opportunities for more prestigious and higher-paying employment options. However, most will never accomplish this leap, since near-minimum wages, labor instability, and long hours prevent them from obtaining the further qualifications necessary to achieve this upward mobility (e.g., Coe 2019; Ray 2018). The overrepresentation of women of color in service work is an example of what Saidiya Hartman (2007) has called "the afterlife of slavery"; women of color are seen as "naturally" suited for the low-status and intimate labor of caring for white(r) and wealthier households and shut out of more lucrative professional opportunities (Boris and Parreñas 2010; Fraser 2016; Glenn 1992; Roberts 1997).

America's low-wage service sector thus relies upon the reproduction of an economically marginalized, feminized, and racialized workforce—one face of what Guy Standing (2014) has famously labeled the "precariat"—who labor in low-paid, unstable, and insecure jobs with little claim to benefits from either employers or the state. As such, the service sector is a prime exemplar of "precarious work," defined as "work that is *uncertain, unstable*, and *insecure* and in which *employees bear the risks* of work (as opposed to businesses or the government) and *receive limited social benefits and statutory entitlements*" (Kalleberg 2018, 3, italics in original). As we will see, vulnerability to precarity has both economic and temporal dimensions.

"Flexible Labor" and Its Discontents: Temporal Precarity, Inequality, and (Ill) Health

The expansion of the 24/7 service economy has profoundly shaped the temporal landscape of life and labor, both in the United States and globally, requiring that low-wage workers make themselves available to labor on weekends and outside standard nine-to-five workdays. It is they who staff retail and grocery stores, serve early-morning cappuccinos to commuters or clean office buildings at night, and field call-center calls from customers half a world and multiple time zones away (Jacobs and Gerson 2004; Mankekar and Gupta 2019; Presser 2003). In the United States, these positions are often viewed as temporary jobs for young people or as stepping stones to higher-earning professions. However, many workers in this sector are adults with dependents who face permanent employment in low-wage positions (National Women's Law Center 2014; Newman 2009; Ray 2018).

Research on service work has focused in particular on the economic aspects of precarity, in which low and uncertain wages destabilize workers' well-being and ability to plan for the future (Edin and Lein 1997; Kalleberg 2009; Newman 2009; Ray 2018). More recently, scholars have called attention to the deleterious effects of temporal precarity, whereby the inability to control or predict one's time jeopardizes workers' economic and emotional well-being (Carrillo et al. 2017; Henly, Shaefer, and Waxman 2006; Kalleberg 2018; Snyder 2016). In industries such as food service and retail, companies tightly tie staffing to expected demand, containing costs by scheduling the minimum number of employees for the least number of hours without alienating customers by long lines and wait times (Henly, Shaefer, and Waxman 2006; Lambert 2008). Common scheduling practices include cutting short or canceling shifts if demand is slower than predicted, even if the employee has already invested time and money to come to work in the expectation of a full shift's pay. In some states, companies are legally permitted to mandate unpaid "on call time," which requires employees to clear their schedules and make themselves ready to work if called in at the last minute, disrupting plans and incurring expenses (such as childcare) in the expectation of a shift that might never materialize (Kantor 2014; Scheiber 2015). Even low-wage service workers with apparently stable schedules, like health aides who provide in-home care services, are vulnerable to temporal precarity since their cases can be abruptly canceled if a client dies, loses health insurance coverage, or goes to the hospital. Such events can mean a loss of income of weeks or even months until the aide is reassigned (Buch 2018; Coe 2019). By providing work only when there is demand rather than guaranteeing a predictable living wage, companies maximize profit margins and devolve responsibility for economic survival to the employees themselves (Guendelsberger 2019; Hacker 2006; Snyder 2016; Stuesse 2016). In the process, they produce a temporally precarious workforce whose ability to plan their lives and to care for themselves, their families, and their households is severely constrained.

Attention to temporal precarity thus highlights how individuals and collectives are unevenly exposed to risk through different expressions of corporate temporal governance. Low-wage service employers often tout work flexibility as a benefit that allows employees to schedule work around their other commitments. However, by contrast with the positively valued "flex-work" policies that have become increasingly prevalent in professional settings, especially after the COVID-19 pandemic that postdates this research, flexible scheduling in the low-wage service sector usually means flexibility for employers and *instability* for workers (Henly, Shaefer, and Waxman 2006). Temporally precarious work, like other forms of rotating and nonstandard shift work, produces acute disarticulations with other biological and social rhythms; a number of studies have shown the toll of disrupted sleeping and eating patterns, financial stress, and broken social commitments on the physical, social, and psychological well-being of workers (Henly and Lambert 2014; Mankekar and Gupta 2019; Snyder 2016; Winant 2021). An important investigative article in the *New York Times* (Kantor 2014) revealed the devastating impact of unpredictable and last-minute scheduling practices on one Starbucks employee, whose inability to predict her weekly income, schedule, or childcare needs jeopardized her ability to care for her young son and led to the eventual dissolution of her relationship with her partner. (In response, Starbucks vowed to provide more schedule stability and predictability for its employees). Research demonstrates that temporal precarity is even more likely than poverty to be cited as a factor in workers' stress and unhappiness (Henly and Lambert 2014; Schneider and Harknett 2019), and that workers would prefer to take jobs with lower earnings and stable schedules over positions that offer higher pay but unpredictable schedules (Halpin and Smith 2017; Mas and Pallais 2017).

In their physical, social, and emotional suffering, temporally precarious workers thus endure what sociologist Benjamin Snyder describes as the disorders of "routinely exposing the body to certain necessary desynchronizations" (2016, 182; see also Mankekar and Gupta 2019). These analyses demonstrate the necessity of expanding concerns with temporal precarity beyond unpredictable and unstable scheduling to engage a larger body of scholarship that situates precarity as "the politically induced condition in which certain populations suffer from failing social and economic networks, . . . becoming differentially exposed to injury, violence, and death" (Butler 2009, ii; see also Tsing 2015). This framing makes clear that temporal precarity is a form of structural violence that impedes both individual and collective access to the economic, social, and psychological conditions necessary for well-being.

Yet job-related temporal precarity rarely happens in isolation, since those people most subject to rigid and punitive forms of temporal governance at the workplace are also more likely to experience lack of control over time in other contexts as well. In tracing the effects of temporal inequalities on pregnant service sector workers, my analysis focuses on the intersection of three particular domains of time: *labor time*, the highly regimented and regulated temporal regimes typical of most service workplaces; *clinical time*,[3] the hierarchical and bureaucratic organization of time in medical settings; and *gestational time*,[4] which I define as the development of pregnancy over time, as well as the quotidian cyclical rhythms of the pregnant body itself. Focusing on the dilemmas and decisions as pregnant service workers navigate the disarticulations and conflicts between the temporal structures of labor and safety net prenatal care makes clear that reproduction is not only shaped by processes that take place *over* time. Reproductive experiences and outcomes are also produced through forms of temporal governance that reflect and reproduce the unequal social value assigned to different people's time, bodies, and labor, both productive and reproductive. As we will see, pregnant service workers absorb the all-too-frequent desynchronizations between labor, clinical, and gestational time in and through their bodies, with potentially injurious effects on their reproductive well-being.

Seeking Prenatal Care: Temporal Inequities and Reproductive Health Disparities in New York City

The United States has long ranked below most industrialized countries in maternal and infant health indicators. Between 1993 and 2015, however, national maternal mortality rates actually rose from an estimated 16.9 deaths per 100,000 live births to 26.4 per 100,000, giving the United States the worst maternal outcomes of all "developed" countries (e.g., GBD 2015 Maternal Mortality Collaborators 2016). In 2016 New York City's Department of Health released a much-anticipated report on racial disparities in the city's maternal and infant mortality rates. Its findings were shocking. Although overall maternal mortality rates had remained relatively stagnant since 2010, the racial gap had almost doubled. Maternal mortality rates for non-Hispanic Black women were twelve times higher than those of non-Hispanic white women, a disparity three to four times greater than those of the nation at large (New York City Department of Health and Mental Hygiene 2015, 2016). These stark disparities in reproductive outcomes affected Black women across all economic and educational statuses, with Black college-educated women more likely to suffer life-threatening complications than white women who had never graduated from high school (New York City Department of Health and Mental Hygiene 2016). Moreover, despite decreasing rates of infant mortality overall, the mortality rate for Black infants was still more than twice as high as that of white infants, and Black infants were more likely to be born prematurely than any other racial/ethnic group (New York City Bureau of Vital Statistics 2021; March of Dimes 2021).

Although Black and brown communities (and their allies) in New York City had long denounced conditions that led to poorer reproductive outcomes (e.g., Mullings and Wali 2001), these reports provoked urgently needed public debate about stratified reproduction and the pernicious effects of structural, institutional, and medical racism on Black women and infants. Communities of color and their supporters demonstrated through street protests, petitions, and social media, directly connecting their poorer pregnancy and birth outcomes to negligent and discriminatory medical care as well as entrenched racial and gender inequalities. Media stories spotlighted systemic inequalities and "diagnostic lapses" (D. Davis 2019) in Black women's encounters with prenatal and obstetric care, with several focusing directly on safety net hospitals serving Black-majority neighborhoods in Brooklyn (including Beaumont) where rates of maternal mortality and morbidity were far higher than rates in the rest of New York City (Martin and Montagne 2017; Mogul 2017; Villarosa 2018; Waldman 2017). Tracing causality beyond individual behaviors and risk factors, these reports pointed to the direct effects of medical racism and race-based resource disparities as well as to the cumulative burden of stress caused by structural violence and racism that prematurely ages and injures Black bodies (Geronimus 1992; Lu and Halfon 2003).

These reproductive disparities are the direct legacies of America's histories of slavery and settler colonialism, made concrete in "skewed life chances, limited access to health and education, [and] premature death" (Hartman 2007, 6; see also D. Davis 2019; Geronimus 1992; Hoberman 2012; Mullings 2005; Roberts 1997). One avenue through which these violent histories are perpetuated is through racist forms of reproductive governance, which Lynn Morgan and Elizabeth Roberts define as "the mechanisms through which different historical configurations of actors—such as state, religious, and international financial institutions, NGOs, and social movements—use legislative controls, economic inducements, moral injunctions, direct coercion, and ethical incitements to produce, monitor, and control reproductive behaviours and population practices" (2012, 243). In the United States, this has resulted in a deeply unequal reproductive landscape and the selective distribution, or even denial, of resources that low-income communities and communities of color need to bear and care for dependents in safe and dignified environments (Ross and Solinger 2017). Analyses show that states with a larger Black population tend to spend less than other states on cash assistance to impoverished mothers and children, are less likely to have paid sick or family leave, and impose more restrictions on eligibility and access to safety net programs, such as Medicaid-covered healthcare and subsidized childcare for low-income working parents (Badger et al. 2022). As advocates for reproductive justice point out, such practices exacerbate racial disparities in economic status and social well-being, negatively shaping the conditions for the reproduction of Black and brown children and communities (Briggs 2017; Roberts 1997; Ross and Solinger 2017).

Seen in this context, New York City provides a relatively robust set of social and safety net programs for low-income pregnant working people. New York State's expansion of Medicaid under the 2010 Affordable Care Act guarantees Medicaid-covered healthcare to all pregnant people, including undocumented immigrants, up to 233 percent of the federal poverty line until sixty days after the end of the pregnancy (extended to twelve months in 2021). In 2014 New York City also implemented the Pregnant Workers Fairness Act and the Paid Sick Leave Law (expanded in 2018 and renamed the Paid Safe and Sick Leave Act; I refer to the act using the current name throughout the book). Currently, the Paid Safe and Sick Leave Act guarantees all workers at companies with a net annual profit of over one million dollars the right to accrue up to forty hours of paid time off per year (and fifty-six hours for those with more than one hundred employees) to use when they are sick, seeking medical care, or caring for a sick dependent, while the Pregnant Workers Fairness Act mandates a suite of protections for pregnant and postpartum workers at companies that employ four or more workers. In addition to requiring that employers grant requests for "reasonable accommodations" to pregnant women whose jobs require heavy lifting or long periods of standing, the act guarantees them the right to unpaid time off for prenatal or postpartum care, additional breaks to sit down, eat or drink, or use the restroom, as well as time to pump breastmilk and to recover from childbirth, as long as this does not represent an "undue burden" for the employer. Importantly, this legislation encompasses groups of workers who have historically been excluded from labor laws; both acts cover undocumented workers while the Paid Safe and Sick Leave Act includes protections for domestic workers, who are often carved out of workplace protections given their location within employers' "private" domestic space.

The centrality of time protections in both pieces of legislation underscores a growing recognition of the ways that temporal governance in the workplace influences apparently "private" reproductive behaviors, experiences, and outcomes. Even in the context of the United States' limited protections, middle- and upper-middle-class professionals usually have the relative luxury of salaried employment and stable schedules, paid time off, and the ability to negotiate flexible and work-from-home days that gives them a measure of control over their own labor time (Boushey 2016; Goodin 2009; Jacobs and Gerson 2004). Although a prenatal appointment scheduled during a workday may be an inconvenience, most can take a long lunch hour, come into work late, or leave early without losing income. By contrast, service workers' wages are connected to industrial "clock time" (Thompson 1967) in ways that directly penalize them for time spent obtaining prenatal care. Since service workers are usually not permitted to arrive late or leave a shift early, those unable to reconcile this conflict must choose between delaying care or giving up a full shift—a whole day's pay—to attend a medical appointment. At the same time, since low-wage service workers frequently depend upon safety net services for healthcare, they are also exposed to the delays and bureaucracy of clinical time where they can expend countless hours waiting for slow and often indifferent government services (Auyero 2012). Data from the New York State Department of Health (2013) show that non-Hispanic Black women in New York City are three times more likely than non-Hispanic white women to access prenatal care "late" (at or after thirteen weeks of gestation) or not at all. Although the report did not include reasons for delaying care, research in other US sites has pointed to a number of barriers to prenatal care for low-resource Black and brown women, including lack of affordable and accessible healthcare, experiences of provider hostility, and inability to take time off for prenatal appointments (Daniels, Noe, and Mayberry 2006; Gemmill et al. 2019).

The temporal nature of pregnancy and the moral freighting of prenatal care brings these disjunctures among labor, clinical, and gestational time into sharp focus. Pregnancy is by definition time-limited; if a pregnant person is to obtain "timely" care (before thirteen weeks of gestation), medical appointments cannot be constantly put off to another week or month. Prenatal appointments also follow a predetermined and closely monitored schedule—for low-risk patients, once a month for the first two trimesters, twice a month for the third trimester, and weekly in the last month—meaning that even routine care requires a considerable investment of time. In the arc of gestational time, temporal conflicts between work and prenatal care that are manageable in the first trimester may thus become acute by the end of the pregnancy. There are also specific social, cultural, and emotional pressures to attend prenatal care that set it apart from most routine medical appointments. Scholars of reproduction have shown how women enact cultural ideologies of "good" and "responsible" motherhood through adherence to the requirements of prenatal care or even pre-pregnancy care (Andaya 2014;

Georges 2008; Waggoner 2017). They may also enjoy certain aspects of the clinical encounter, such as the sonogram appointments in which their fetus is made "visible" to them, and actively seek care in these moments (Mitchell and Georges 1997; Mitchell 2001).

Given higher rates of late or no prenatal care, as well as poorer reproductive outcomes as a population, low-income women and women of color are particularly targeted in public health messaging about the urgency of prioritizing their pregnancy over other claims to their time. Yet despite these exhortations, low-wage service workers, who comprise a significant portion of this "at-risk" group, are less likely than employees in other types of sectors to benefit from paid time from work to attend prenatal care or to care for themselves and their newborns after birth (A Better Balance 2021a). With few protections, they must make fraught and anxiety-ridden decisions to delay prenatal care, give up a needed shift to keep their medical appointment (thus accepting loss of income as an inevitable cost of seeking care), or return to work weeks or even days after giving birth. They are also vulnerable to other punitive forms of temporal governance when employers or supervisors deny requests for additional time to use the bathroom, eat, or sit down on the grounds that such exceptions disrupt the carefully regulated rhythms of work in the service workplace (Silver-Greenberg and Kitroeff 2018).

These temporal inequities push the frame of analysis beyond that of individual gestational time to highlight the broader social and generational contexts in which reproduction takes place (Ginsburg and Rapp 1995). A confluence of vulnerabilities means that low-income Black and brown women are more likely than other groups to occupy positions in which they experience "time seizures" (A. Cooper 2015) by both states and capital, and to be subjected to structures of time that they feel devalue them, their time, and their well-being. For them, the temporal governance typical of low-wage service work constrains access to the routine prenatal care that might help to detect chronic and emerging health concerns. At the same time, long waits and rushed medical encounters in frequently overextended safety net hospitals mean that patients do not always receive appropriate and timely diagnosis, monitoring, and intervention, while time-pressured providers may be less likely to engage in the kinds of clinical interactions that patients perceive as "caring."

Critical attention to pregnant workers' experience of the (dis)articulation between the temporal regimes of low-wage service workplaces and the safety net health institutions in which they seek care thus offers a new perspective on how racial and class inequalities are reproduced in and through bodies and social institutions. This is not to claim a direct causality between time and rates of maternal morbidity and mortality. Rather, bringing time into the analysis illustrates how forms of temporal governance and site-specific temporal regimes can become key vectors through which racialized patient populations, as well as the medical staff who work in racialized systems of safety net healthcare, encounter the lesser value assigned to their time, bodies, and labor. In this context, as advocates for reproductive and temporal justice make clear, social struggles to improve health and labor conditions for low-wage pregnant people involve not only efforts to ensure the survival and well-being of individual pregnancies. They also entail a radical rethinking of the broader social structures, practices, and policies through which inequality is reproduced through and over time.

Mapping the Field

This research has spanned many years during which the concerns that animate this book—access to healthcare, racial inequality, reproductive justice, and workers' rights, among others—have catapulted to the forefront of public and political debate. My fieldwork concluded in 2016, before the world-changing events of the COVID-19 pandemic and its devastating effects on New York City, but the struggles around time and care for low-wage pregnant workers have only become more critical in the (post)pandemic era. The book draws on more than a decade of research, during which I have tracked local, state, and national policy discussions around labor, prenatal care, and paid parental leave in my adopted city of New York. While conducting research "at home" in New York City complicates efforts to clearly periodize time in "the field," the most intensive part of this research took place between September 2015 and August 2016, during which I conducted interviews and ethnographic observation twice a week at the low-risk prenatal clinic of a public safety net hospital that I call Beaumont Hospital. The definition of "safety net" is broad, and a systematic review of studies published between 2009 and 2018 found broad variability in definitions and operationalization of the term. High loads of Medicaid and uncompensated care emerged as a widely used conceptual category, as well as a moral commitment to providing care regardless of patient ability to pay, and I follow this definition here (Hefner et al. 2021). Typically located in low-income areas with few non-hospital-based medical offices, safety net hospitals face chronic budgetary shortfalls from both local and federal governments (Chokshi, Chang, and Wilson 2016; Goldstein 2022; Hadley et al. 2008).

My arrival at Beaumont was serendipitous. As I began developing the outlines of this research, I had the great good fortune to meet a provider whom I call Dr. Silva, a politically and socially engaged ob-gyn and a fellow parent in our then two-year-old children's daycare, who facilitated my entrée into the obstetrics and gynecology department at Beaumont Hospital. It proved a fertile ground for this research. A 2013 community needs assessment reported that Beaumont serves neighborhoods that are 82 percent Black and 12 percent Latinx, with approximately a quarter speaking a primary language other than English. Poverty levels in its catchment area are about 20 percent higher than in New York City as a whole, despite high levels of employment. The large majority of Beaumont's patients are covered by public insurance (Medicaid and Medicare) and many lack health insurance due to documentation status, since federal laws prohibit undocumented migrants from obtaining public or private insurance coverage. In fact, uninsured patients make up 39 percent of Beaumont's outpatient visits and 35 percent of its emergency room visits, considerably higher than the citywide average for public hospitals (19 percent and 20 percent, respectively).[5]

At the time of my research, providers estimated that the hospital managed about three thousand births per year, a number considered only moderate for a New York City public hospital (and which declined in subsequent years as Trump-era anti-immigrant policies discouraged migrant pregnant women from seeking prenatal care). The prenatal clinic, like Beaumont at large, served various kinds of patients. While many arrived in good health and with only minor economic or social stresses, others presented with chronic and sometimes poorly managed health problems that affected their well-being during pregnancy. Some were unstably housed and a few were in dire economic straits, which often led to higher rates of late or intermittent prenatal care. Given its location amidst highly transnational neighborhoods, providers not infrequently saw immigrant women in late stages of pregnancy with no history of prenatal care in the United States, although some had been attending care in their home countries.

Recruitment of study participants took place in Beaumont's low-risk prenatal clinic, reflecting hospital administrators' perception that this population would have fewer "confounding" medical factors (as well as, I suspect, a concern that my interviews could hold up patient flow for the busy providers in the high-risk clinic). This boundary was a porous one, albeit largely unidirectional; several of the women I first interviewed in the low-risk clinic were moved into the high-risk clinic later in their pregnancy after being diagnosed with conditions such as hypertension or gestational diabetes. The increased medical monitoring and testing associated with their various conditions made the temporal conflicts between work and prenatal care even more acute for them than for the bulk of my "low-risk" interlocutors.

I began fieldwork by simply sitting with patients in the clinic waiting room, tracking wait times to appointments, and engaging in casual conversations with patients and passing staff. As my relationships with clinic members deepened, I was invited to sit behind the reception desk, which provided valuable insights as I witnessed interactions between staff and patients, chatted with the receptionists and providers, and answered questions from patients who mistook me for a clinic member, despite my efforts to correct this impression. At first, I viewed the waiting room primarily as an opportune location for recruitment. Yet as Aditya Bharadwaj (2016) has noted, medical waiting rooms make fertile sites for ethnographic research. They are a liminal space between the clinic's "inside" and "outside," where interactions between patients, staff, and the workings of clinical bureaucracy publicly unfold and where often implicit norms and perceived transgressions are made evident. Although this research was not intended as an ethnography of an institution, my observations in Beaumont's hallways and waiting rooms—particularly with respect to the length of time that women spent waiting—were critical to my understanding of how the disjunctive temporal regimes of work and clinical care shaped reproductive temporalities, constraining people's ability to care for themselves and others.

After this initial period of participant-observation, I began recruiting patients by following the daily sessions on breastfeeding and infant care, run in the clinic waiting room by a jovial medical educator, with an informational presentation about New York City's then recently passed Paid Safe and Sick Leave and Pregnant Workers Fairness Acts. At its conclusion, I provided patients with policy handouts and resources, answered questions, and invited interested women to participate in this study. In all, I conducted semi-structured interviews with fifty-five pregnant women, all over eighteen years of age and employed in the service sector. As a note on terminology, I recognize that not all pregnant and birthing people identify as women, although all participants, when asked for their preference, indicated that they used female pronouns. In this book, I use both "women" and "pregnant people" or "pregnant workers"; my use of the term "women" is thus not intended to circumscribe the wide range of gendered reproductive experience but rather to serve as a shorthand for particular reproductive and social positions within historical and cultural configurations of power.

The demographics of my sample reflect the general composition of the hospital population: all except three (who identified as Latina/Hispanic) described themselves as Black, although those who were recent immigrants tended to also respond to questions about their racial/ethnic identification with their country of origin, perhaps reflecting their discomfort with US racial categories. Nineteen were born in the United States, thirteen in Jamaica, seven in Guyana, seven in smaller islands in the Anglophone Caribbean, six in Haiti, and one each in the Dominican Republic, Sierra Leone, and Côte d'Ivoire. Eighteen were aged between eighteen and twenty-four at the time of the interview, twenty-four were between twenty-five and thirty years of age, five were between thirty-one and thirty-six years of age, and eight were thirty-six years old or older. More than half (twenty-six) were expecting their first child. Participants worked in a variety of service positions, from domestic work to beauty salons to food service, but the majority were employed in three principal fields: twenty-two in healthcare, as home health aides, personal care aides, or aides in nursing homes; eight in retail; and eight in food service. The number of health workers in my sample (close to half) illustrates the importance of healthcare as an employment sector in New York City. Eighteen percent of the workforce in Brooklyn and a full 25 percent in the Bronx is employed in healthcare or social assistance, some of the highest proportions in the country (Winant 2021). Finally, twenty-nine women described unpredictable and fluctuating schedules while twenty-six, primarily in healthcare, reported relatively stable weekly schedules.

Participants often had difficulty estimating their annual income due to high variability in working hours, but most indicated that they made approximately $25,000 per year or less. None made more than $15 per hour, with almost half reporting near-minimum wage ($10 or less per hour; the minimum wage in New York City at the time was $8.75 per hour). Underemployment was the norm: all but two worked fewer than forty hours a week, with some reporting fewer than twenty-five hours per week. All qualified for WIC (Special Nutrition Program for Women,

Infants, and Children)[6] to supplement their food budgets, and several also qualified for SNAP benefits[7] or welfare assistance. All but one was enrolled in Medicaid.[8] Of these, thirty-eight had been covered by Medicaid prior to their pregnancy and sixteen had been enrolled into Medicaid through state laws that extend Medicaid coverage to undocumented pregnant people as well as uninsured pregnant people whose incomes are higher than the regular Medicaid threshold. Eleven of the women who were uninsured prior to pregnancy were born outside the United States, suggesting that their lack of health insurance may have been due to their status as undocumented immigrants. However, I had decided early in my research that I would not ask participants to disclose their immigration status; while some volunteered this information during interviews, I was careful not to ask any questions that could implicate them. Finally, since I recruited exclusively at a prenatal clinic, my research sample was only comprised of women who did access prenatal care, even if intermittently. Although interviews with pregnant people who for various reasons had never accessed prenatal care would have made a fascinating addition to the study, the difficulties of locating and recruiting these participants would have been considerable.

Interview questions clustered around three main topics. The first addressed workplace temporal regimes and governance, including scheduling practices and typical work schedules and hours, policies around absences and switching shifts, strategies for scheduling and attending prenatal care around work, and experiences of working while pregnant. The second topic asked about prenatal care at Beaumont, especially participants' ability to schedule appointments at convenient times, typical wait times before being seen by a provider, and clinical interactions. The final topic sought to investigate realms of policy and practice by inquiring about participants' familiarity with the Pregnant Workers Fairness Act and the Paid Safe and Sick Leave Act, as well as their experience with requesting pregnancy-related accommodations, such as time off to attend prenatal care. Although I collected basic demographic data, such as hourly wage and general household income and composition, I avoided delving too deeply into domestic arrangements or the income-generating activities of other household members, especially partners. Acutely aware that low-income women accessing state services face constant intrusions into private domains, particularly with respect to the presence and occupation of romantic partners, I did not wish to duplicate these forms of government surveillance and invasion of privacy (Bridges 2017). In many cases, these topics arose organically as women discussed strategies for managing work schedules or the temporal and financial pressures that they felt as low-wage workers.

Interviews took place in a private office in the hospital while women were waiting for their appointments and were remunerated with a $15 Metrocard valid on New York City's subway and bus system. I conducted all of the interviews and audiorecorded them with the participant's consent. If consent for audiorecording was not provided, I took extensive fieldnotes immediately after the interview. Although I never asked for reasons for refusal, those participants who requested that I not audiorecord their interviews often confided concerns about their status as undocumented migrants or as recipients of welfare benefits. Underscoring the fluid boundaries between research and surveillance, such interactions were an important reminder of anthropology's historic complicity with projects of state governance and the necessity for the discipline's ongoing reckoning with the entwined histories of colonial power and the production of knowledge (Jobson 2020). As a small step in this direction, I respected those moments when women's pauses suggested a desire for privacy, and tried to provide resources and support for participants needing information about their rights or help navigating the city's system for lodging complaints against employers. I describe one of these instances in the final chapter.

Since the primary intention of this research was to examine the effects of service sector employment on access to prenatal healthcare, I did not systematically recruit providers. However, I did formally interview seven prenatal care providers (three obstetricians and four midwives) who worked in several public hospitals in New York City, including Beaumont, as well as a policy advocate for home health aides. I also had many informal conversations with staff at Beaumont, from providers to receptionists, and, over the years of research and writing, I engaged in discussions and conversations with many more from an array of New York City hospitals.

In the initial design of this project, I had hoped to re-interview women after the birth of their children to track whether, and under what conditions, women returned to paid labor. However, like many other researchers working among low-income and often (transnationally) mobile populations, I found this far more difficult than I had anticipated. In my attempts to follow up with participants, I encountered disconnected phone numbers, left unreturned messages on numerous voicemails, and fielded return phone calls in which women promised to get back to me with a convenient interview time—soon, but not now. As discouraging as this sometimes was, as a mother myself, I also very much appreciated that life with a new baby can feel exhausting and overwhelming, even for women with stable economic situations, and that follow-up interviews were simply not a priority. These setbacks were balanced by encounters with women whom I saw month after month in their prenatal care, providing the opportunity to follow up about their experiences of managing working and prenatal care as their pregnancies progressed. A few relationships forged during this time lasted beyond the birth of their child, as we kept in touch through Facebook, texts, and occasional visits.

Beyond my work at Beaumont, New York City proved a dynamic place for this research. In addition to the 2014 Paid Safe and Sick Leave Act and the Pregnant Workers Fairness Act, New York State passed the Paid Family Leave Act in 2016, making it, as of 2023, one of just eleven states and the District of Columbia that guarantee eligible workers paid time off to care for close relatives. Although it did not go into effect until 2018, well after the conclusion of the ethnographic portion of my research, the advocacy and lobbying efforts surrounding its passage also informed this study. Between 2014 and 2023, I attended conferences, webinars, and talks (many organized by the excellent legal advocacy organization A Better Balance), and collected an ever-expanding archive of newspaper, television, and web-based materials on topics from prenatal and maternal healthcare in New York City to working conditions for pregnant workers and caregivers. I was also extremely fortunate to be invited at an early stage of this research to attend working meetings of an eminent group of work-life researchers, hosted at Columbia University, that were critical in elucidating the wider policy context.

Until the COVID-19 pandemic sent New York City into lockdown in mid-March 2020, I participated in rallies and informational meetings held by advocates for birth justice for Black and brown women, as well as by activists fighting for an increase in the minimum wage to $15 per hour. The pandemic, as well as the growing prominence of the Black Lives Matter movement, forced a broader public acknowledgment that much of the workforce newly designated as "essential" were Black and brown women in low-wage and often low-status service jobs who came from communities that were disproportionately sick and dying from COVID-19. Although this research was conducted before these world-altering events, the critical debates that they provoked foregrounded concerns about time, labor, inequality, and social questions of care that deeply informed the final conceptualization and writing of the book. It is my hope that this research will contribute in some small way to these struggles for social justice.

Chapter Outline

The next chapter, "Service Labor and Temporal Governance in the 'City That Never Sleeps,'" situates the ethnography more specifically in New York City and examines the perception of service work as low-skill, low-status, racialized, and gendered labor. It describes the various regimes of labor time typical in different types of service work, as well as the local and federal policies that govern corporate reach over workers' time. It thus reveals how the intersection of corporate temporal governance with limited forms of state protection produces a temporally precarious and constantly available service workforce.

Chapter 2, "Working While Pregnant: Conflicts between Labor, Clinical, and Gestational Time," examines the disconnect between gestational time and the time discipline of low-wage labor. Drawing on pregnant workers' experiences of managing the physical demands of service labor, it traces how the racialized temporal logic of service work is refracted in and through workers' pregnant bodies. As we will see, for many women, the requirement to maintain the tempo of labor time was sharply at odds with the arc of gestational time and the needs of their pregnant bodies. At the same time, pregnant workers were often forced to navigate conflicts between the rigidity of labor time and the ponderous pace of clinical time in their efforts to access routine prenatal care.

Chapter 3, "Clinical Time and Racialized Inequality in Safety Net Prenatal Care," draws in more detail on my ethnographic observations at Beaumont Hospital's prenatal clinic. Through close attention to patient and provider experience, it demonstrates how the racialized systems of value that chronically underfund safety net health institutions contribute to temporal structures that produce experiences of time pressure for providers and time "wastage" for patients. Tracing the frustration and tensions as both providers and patients interpret these temporal regimes as a lack of care for their well-being, it shows how inequality is instantiated and experienced through racialized and classed structures of clinical time.

A key concern of this research was to ascertain whether pregnant service workers were aware of the newly passed Pregnant Workers Fairness Act and the Paid Safe and Sick Leave Act, and the degree to which they anticipated that these new rights would benefit them. The final chapter, "Cosmologies of Care: Temporal Justice and the Politics of Value," situates struggles over productive and reproductive time within a growing popular, scholarly, and policy discourse on the politics of care and value. As we will see, rather than using the language of rights, the women I interviewed interpreted supervisors' willingness to make accommodations for pregnant workers within a discourse of care in which higher-ups "cared"—or did not—about them and their future children. By contrast, advocates for New York State's Paid Family Leave Act expanded the definition of care to encompass not only interpersonal relationships but the obligations of states to protect citizens' time to care. In so doing, they argued that time was central to social justice.

The book's conclusion provides an update to the post-COVID-19 policy landscape, highlighting the social debates around time, care, and social value laid bare by the pandemic, the Black Lives Matter movement, and advocacy for labor and reproductive justice. These collective struggles for temporal justice make clear that what is at stake is not only the effort to improve individual lives through reproductive and labor policy. Raising urgent questions about how we value care in a deeply unequal society, they also invoke possibilities for conceiving new cultural and social futures for us all (Ginsburg and Rapp 1995; Ross and Solinger 2017).

1

Service Labor and Temporal Governance in the "City That Never Sleeps"

Around seven o'clock every weekday morning in the Brooklyn neighborhood in which I lived during my fieldwork, a quotidian temporal labor flow began to take shape. Slowly at first, and then with increasing frequency, groups of women began to emerge from the subway stations that linked this neighborhood to less affluent areas deeper into Brooklyn and Queens. Noticeable in this largely white residential zone, most were Black and brown women who, moving singly or in chatting pairs, called goodbyes to each other as they dispersed along the leafy tree-lined streets to their jobs as caregivers for the neighborhood's young and elderly. About eight o'clock, a counterflow began as earlier-rising neighborhood residents departed to the business and financial districts that housed their jobs in law, finance, technology, and governance. With children safely taken into the care of schools, daycares, and nannies, parents dashed for the crowded subways holding to-go cups of coffee and bagel sandwiches. In the evening, this pattern reversed. Commuters streamed from subway stations, pausing on their walk home to pick up dry cleaning from the local laundromat or purchase food for dinner. Only when relieved of their charges for the day could babysitters and caregivers begin their own trip home to resume their caregiving and domestic responsibilities, which of necessity were pushed to the early hours of the morning before others were awake or late into the evening.

This largely unremarked rhythm of life and work in the (upper) middle-class areas of New York City, as in many cities in the United States, is a direct consequence of the explosive growth of both professional and low-wage service occupations in the late twentieth and early twenty-first centuries. Despite the differences in remuneration and status between these two poles of service employment, an important body of scholarship has shown that the lack of the social value attributed to the latter is rooted in sexist, racist, and classist structures rather than in any inherent properties of the work itself (e.g., Boris and Parreñas 2010; Coe 2019; Ehrenreich and Hochschild 2003). Tasks such as cleaning, preparing food, and caregiving have long been assigned to the culturally devalued domain of unpaid women in the home, where capitalist logic holds that its inability to produce profit makes it inferior to waged labor (A. Davis 1981). Affective labor, also culturally gendered as feminine, is integral to service work: child caregivers and home health care workers are charged not only with fulfilling the tasks of cleaning, feeding, and dressing their charges, but also with carrying out such duties with caring and empathy, while employees in other service sectors must interact cheerfully and helpfully with customers, defuse conflict, and listen to customers' confidences during haircuts and pedicures (Boris and Parreñas 2010; Hochschild 2003). When such work moves into the paid sector, it retains its association with the gendered reproductive labor, both affective and physical, that is assumed to be the "natural" domain of women (Ehrenreich and Hochschild 2003). Scholars have also called attention to the racialized nature of low-wage service work, pointing to the direct link between the racial hierarchies produced by colonialism and slavery and the disproportionate number of Black and brown people employed in this low-status and poorly remunerated labor (Glenn 1992; Rollins 1985).

Gender and racial stereotypes, in which reproductive labor is seen as feminized work that comes "naturally" to women (of color), thus serve to bolster popular perceptions of service work as unskilled and undeserving of recognition, economic or otherwise (Fraser 2016). Yet assumptions about the lack of skill required of service work rest on the failure—or refusal—to recognize the expertise required to perform these tasks well. In her study of home health care workers, Elana Buch (2018) describes how the aides whom her elderly informants considered "good workers" were those who were able to anticipate their clients' needs so thoroughly that they needed no instruction. The practiced invisibility of their labor obscured the competence that "good" workers bring to their jobs, relegating the knowledge gained through years of experience to the domain of "women's nature" and bolstering beliefs about home health care as unskilled work.

This chapter contributes to this intersectional analysis of service labor by showing how both state and corporate temporal governance reflect and reproduce gendered, racialized, and classed systems of value. It outlines the forms of labor time that structure work in different service sectors, as well as how the temporal governance typical of low-wage service workplaces devalues workers and their time by treating both as constantly available and imminently disposable resources. The chapter concludes with an overview of local and federal policies from New York City's Pregnant Workers Fairness Act and Paid Safe and Sick Leave Act to the federal Family Medical Leave Act (FMLA) that seek, although in sometimes limited ways, to protect workers' time to care for themselves and for their dependents. Despite laudable recent efforts to expand temporal protections, their reach continues to be limited by the structure of low-wage service work and long-standing racial, class, and gender ideologies about the unequal worth of different people's time.

Structures of Labor Time and Temporal Precarity in Service Work

Six days a week, Tanisha Williams wakes at three o'clock in the morning to make her way from her home in central Brooklyn to her 5:00 a.m. shift in a buffet restaurant in Manhattan. Rising at that hour, still more night than morning, gives her time to shower and get ready, pack her daughter's lunch for school, and catch the 4:08 a.m. subway from Brooklyn, which will take her to a connecting subway that transports her to her workplace. She hates her commute. It's dark and frigid in the winter, and in those predawn hours the subway platforms are either deserted or occupied by those whom Tanisha dismissively describes as "crazy people." Unlike New Yorkers with standard working hours who simply arrive at a subway stop and wait for the next train, Tanisha has the subway schedule memorized. If she oversleeps, or is late getting out of the house, she will miss the 4:08 train. At that time of night, they only run every twenty minutes or so; missing it means that she will also miss her connecting subway and will arrive late for her shift. She can't afford to have too many late arrivals on her record. She needs this job.

Tanisha works behind the hot breakfast buffet, serving food to customers and refilling the food trays whenever they run low. The work is constant, physical, and tedious. She is on her feet for her whole shift and must lug the heavy food trays from the kitchen to the buffet station, causing her constant worry about the possibility of miscarriage during her first weeks of pregnancy. She jokes to me that she will never be able to eat bacon and eggs again; during her difficult first trimester, the nausea produced by the inescapable smell of grease often forced her to run, vomiting, to the bathroom or, in more urgent situations, duck out of customers' sight and utilize a trashcan or a Ziploc bag she carried for that express purpose. To her relief, the nausea subsided in her second trimester. Now in her third, new problems have emerged; it is more difficult to lift and carry the hot trays, which she must prop awkwardly against her expanding belly. Fortunately, her co-workers are good about helping when they see her struggling, but she hates to ask them for favors.

Tanisha usually leaves work around midday after the next shift comes in. She picks up her daughter from school at 2:45 p.m., supervises her homework, and then falls asleep at seven or eight o'clock in preparation for her shift the next day. This schedule would be impossible for her as a single mother if not for the fact that she lives with her own mother, who makes sure that Tanisha's daughter gets to school, takes over at night on the evenings that Tanisha falls asleep particularly early—more common now that she is pregnant—and, when possible, covers when Tanisha's daughter is sick or unable to go to school. Although Tanisha is grateful, she is acutely aware of the burden on her mother, who also works in the service sector as a home health aide. She tries not to take advantage.

"I'm tired," she tells me when I interview her as she waits for her prenatal appointment at Beaumont Hospital. "I'm just really, really tired. I can never get used to it, getting up just when your body wants to sleep hard. I don't know if you ever get used to it." I ask whether she plans to return to this job after her baby is born, and she shrugs ruefully. On the one hand, the hours are "horrible," leaving her drained and without time or energy for other activities. On the other, this is a decent job in comparison with some others. She likes her co-workers and makes $10.50 per hour—above New York City's minimum wage, in 2016, of $8.75 per hour—and that is essential for her as she contemplates raising two children with only her mother's help.

A few days later, Mariel Martínez described another temporal regime at her job as a barista just a few blocks across town from Tanisha's workplace. "They're the worst," she declared, her mobile face showing her displeasure at the memory as we talked. "I hate them so much." The topic at hand was so-called "clopenings" (later banned under New York City's Fair Workweek Law), a term popularly used to describe practices of scheduling retail or food-service workers to back-to-back shifts that require them to close a store one evening and open it the next morning. In the coffee shop where Mariel worked, this meant serving the last customer at 11:00 p.m., after which the register had to be closed out, equipment cleaned, and the seating area and bathroom swept, mopped, and tidied up for the next morning. On a good evening, when she was assigned to a shift with hardworking and experienced co-workers, she could be out by midnight or 12:30 at the latest. If they were short-staffed or the shift had new hires who needed instruction and oversight, it could be well past one in the morning by the time they finally locked the store doors. A few short hours later, Mariel would be required to clock in again at 5:00 a.m., ready to open the doors promptly at six to serve early-rising customers.

For Mariel, being scheduled to a clopening began a cascade of negative effects. Getting home or returning to work, normally a relatively quick twenty-five-minute commute on the subway, became a serious obstacle. In the early hours of the morning, subways ran infrequently or, if she was unlucky, not at all. Subway platforms were deserted or, worse, occupied by people under the influence of alcohol and other substances. After being assaulted when emerging from the subway stairs one terrible night, she made sure to carry a can of mace tucked away in her fist and steered clear of anyone loitering in the vicinity. When she could, she much preferred to beg a co-worker who lived close to the store to let her stay rather than make the long and sometimes risky trip home for two to three hours of sleep. Occasionally, when the dark and empty streets felt particularly threatening or her exhaustion was such that she feared falling asleep in the subway car, she would take a taxi home, losing close to half her take-home pay in that twenty-minute ride. "I'm shot the next day," Mariel told me. "When I finish a clopening [usually around 11:00 a.m.], I can't do anything. I've basically pulled an all-nighter, and I'm spent. I try to have my shifts scheduled around school [the community college where she was enrolled], but when I have to work a clopening, I can't go to classes. I just want to go home and sleep." Scheduling practices at her workplace also produced a physical and affective oscillation between exhaustion and anxiety; some weeks, the "clopenings" might be the only hours she worked, forcing her to look for replacement shifts to earn enough to pay her bills.

The dramatic shifts in the temporal structures of work since the mid-twentieth century have been experienced not only by service workers. An analysis of national data found high rates of what the authors call "schedule precarity" among early-career workers, defined as work schedules that are unpredictable, unstable, or unwanted, as measured by variability in hours worked, control over individual schedules, and amount of notice about work schedules (Lambert, Fugiel, and Henly 2014). Yet the study also showed wide variation in employee control over hours, schedules, and advance notice by occupational category. Although the workers whom Lambert and her co-authors call "elite professionals"—lawyers and finance workers, for example—often experience high variability in number of hours worked from week to week, they have more control over when they perform these tasks (arriving at the office early or leaving late, or deciding to leave at 5:00 p.m. but to work over the weekend) and are more able to predict the weeks in which they are likely to experience heavy workloads. Clerical workers, by contrast, have little control over individual schedules but usually have stable hours and set schedules. It is low-paid, hourly-wage workers who clock fewer than forty hours per week who are most likely to experience schedule precarity across all three dimensions: high variability in weekly work hours, little to no input into their work schedules, and short notice about working hours. As we saw in the case of Mary-Ann Joseph in the introduction, some 48 percent of this group reported that they received their schedules with a week or less notice, requiring a frantic reorganization of childcare and other commitments (Carrillo et al. 2017; Henly and Lambert 2014; Lambert, Fugiel, and Henly 2014). Moreover, a full two-thirds of low-wage workers have no control over their starting or ending time, meaning that even quotidian activities such as dropping off a child at school can produce profound temporal conflicts (Boushey 2016; Williams, Blair-Loy, and Berdahl 2013).

Further compounding these inequities in reproductive temporalities, research has shown that some 20 percent of all employed Americans work primarily at nonstandard times, such as nights, weekends, or on a rotating shift, while a third of all households with children include at least one spouse who works nonstandard hours (Presser 2003; Presser and Ward 2011). The increasing prevalence of nonstandard schedules is linked directly to the expansion of the low-wage service sector; in an important early study, Harriet Presser (2003) found that low-wage service sector jobs accounted for nine of the ten employment categories most likely to have nonstandard schedules. Countering claims that workers desire these hours to accommodate other commitments such as education and caregiving, she found that job requirements, rather than personal preference, were the most-cited reason for accepting nonstandard schedules. These temporal structures of low-wage labor reflect and reproduce inequalities of race/ethnicity, class, and gender, since low-income families with young children, particularly female-headed households, are most likely to be subjected to undesired nonstandard and precarious work schedules (Carrillo et al. 2017; Henly and Lambert 2014; Presser 2003). Temporal precarity also has intergenerational effects: emerging research shows that children whose parents are subjected to nonstandard and unstable scheduling report lower levels of happiness and well-being than children whose parents work stable hours (Han and Hart 2022; Luhr, Schneider, and Harknett 2022).

Echoing national findings about the prevalence of nonstandard scheduling in the service sector, only six of the fifty-five women I interviewed worked "standard" hours, defined as a schedule in which most work falls between 8:00 a.m. and 4:00 p.m. on weekdays (Presser 2003). For the remainder, the structure of labor time fell into two archetypical forms that were broadly correlated with occupational sector: the unpredictable and unstable schedules typical of retail and food-service workers and the stable but nonstandard schedules of health and personal care workers. In the first, the number and scheduling of labor hours tended to vary from week to week, often wildly, and workers often received notification only twenty-four to forty-eight hours prior to a shift. Since the predictive scheduling software that many companies use to decide both shift length and number of workers is most accurate with more recent data (for example, tabulating customer demand in the prior week), managers are incentivized to make and post schedules at the last possible moment, making it impossible for workers to plan ahead. The experience of Vanessa Fraser, a forty-one-year-old Guyanese food-service worker pregnant with her fourth child, was typical:

> VANESSA: I get a schedule weekly, which is posted the last day of my work week, which is usually the pay period, and then you have the schedule for next week.
> ELISE: So sometimes you might get your schedule and find out that you have to work the next day?

VANESSA: Yes, that's right. And sometimes, the days change, and you have to be very attentive of which days you have off because it may not be the weekends.

For workers in these industries, scheduling instability and last-minute notification of shifts result in large and small upheavals in other aspects of their lives, from household budgets to childcare coverage. If workers cannot attend a scheduled shift, they can "call out," or notify their supervisors of their inability to report to work that day. However, most workplaces carefully track employee call-outs, and many of the women I interviewed described structures of corporate temporal accounting through which they accrued penalties, known as "points" or "demerits," for calling out without securing a replacement. Since acquiring too many demerits is often grounds for job termination, they usually preferred to assume the additional and unpaid labor of ensuring coverage for shifts that they were unable to work by calling in favors with co-workers or posting advertisements on online and physical company bulletin boards.

In the second type of scheduling, typical in the healthcare sector, work hours were relatively stable from week to week but often included nonstandard nights and weekends. As we will see in the next chapter, more stable schedules did provide workers greater ability to plan for medical appointments and other commitments. Yet this apparent predictability often obscured the temporal precarity produced by longer-term scheduling instability and rampant underemployment. Lucia Germaine, a thirty-five-year-old US-born aide pregnant with her first child, had been removed from her previous case after she told her supervisor that her pregnancy had been designated "high-risk" due to maternal overweight and hypertension. During our interview several weeks after this event, she recognized that her supervisor was concerned about possible risk to her pregnancy and her ability to continue to provide good care, especially since she was often required to lift and move her largely immobilized client. Yet she was indignant that she had not been consulted prior to being removed and that she had still not been reassigned to a permanent case. "They [her supervisor] didn't even ask me if I could do the case!" Lucia exclaimed. "They just called me to tell me I'd been removed. And it's been a month now that I've barely worked. How do they expect me to pay the bills?" Indeed, when I asked her to describe her work hours over the previous month, she detailed dramatic fluctuations from a low of eight hours a week to a high of forty. She explained, "I don't have a steady patient right now. I work four hours, eight hours, ten hours. It all depends on what they [the agency/her supervisor] give me. They'll call me and just let me know the night before if they need me to do something the next day. They told me they don't have any steady case suitable for me right now since I'm pregnant."

Temporal precarity affected even aides fortunate enough to have "steady" cases, since hours for individual clients were largely dictated by Medicaid or Medicare determinations of need. A client might require round-the-clock care, resulting in two twelve-hour shifts five days a week. Alternatively, they might only require a few hours of help with housework and some personal care twice a week, forcing aides to piece together sufficient hours by juggling multiple cases or taking replacement shifts for co-workers who called out. Moreover, aides could never be certain about how long each case would last. Patients could die, worsen to a degree that required a move into nursing home facilities, or improve to the point that insurance would no longer pay for home services. When I asked about schedule variability, Stéphanie Louis, a twenty-one-year-old aide from Haiti pregnant with her first child, reflected, "Sometimes, being a home health aide is almost like a temporary job because you might have a case and then the next month the patient goes to the hospital, and he might not come back. So yeah, they usually change my hours." In such situations, cases could end with little warning to the aide and few guarantees of immediate future work. Unlike their counterparts in most other service sectors, most of the health aides I interviewed said that they had the ability to turn down cases that did not fit their needs. However, there were risks; if they did so, there was no guarantee that they would be offered a more suitable case in its place.

Thus, despite differences in formal scheduling practices across service industries, unpredictability and instability are near-universal characteristics of the temporal regimes of low-wage service work. Some of this instability is produced by workers themselves; even after schedules are posted, last-minute changes are commonplace as employees call out sick or swap shifts in efforts to reconcile work with family and other commitments (Clawson and Gerstel 2014). These practices of employee-driven flexibility are important resources for workers, allowing them some measure of temporal control in workplaces that provide few other accommodations (Henly, Shaefer, and Waxman 2006). Yet they come at a cost, both to the worker and to their labor and social networks. For workers, calling out of a shift means a loss of often needed income. Further, in what Clawson and Gerstel (2014) call the "web of time," practices that permit flexibility for one worker produce instability and unpredictability for others, since replacement workers must bow out of other commitments and make their own last-minute arrangements for transportation, childcare, and other responsibilities. As the web metaphor illustrates, temporal precarity in one life has ripple effects across many other lives as well.

Tanisha's and Mariel's narratives sharply underscore the temporal collisions that the regimes of service work produce with the other patterns of life: circadian rhythms and sleep cycles, transportation, childcare and educational schedules, and the beat of social relationships. For those working nonstandard hours, the demands of a 24/7 global service economy exacerbate temporal disjunctures, forcing workers to align their bodily rhythms and cycles of family and social life to tempos and times that are not their own (Mankekar and Gupta 2019; Presser 2003). For service workers, bringing these patterns into some semblance of alignment means constant physical and emotional effort, as well as a keen awareness of the other schedules—the subway, school timetables, the availability of kin for caregiving—on which they depend to calibrate the delicate balance of their own lives. Such modes of being-in-the-world highlight how temporal precarity forces workers to become "rhythm experts," with deep and hard-won knowledge about the "contingent micromovements of time in the world and the effort needed to synchronize them" (Snyder 2016, 125). This is a skill born of inequality, since those with less power and fewer resources to shape the temporal structures that govern their lives must expend invisible labor in knitting together the patchwork of supports that make possible their survival in systems and hierarchies not of their own making.

(De)Valuing Time: State and Corporate Temporal Governance

Service workers' exposure to temporal precarity underscores their position as what Sarah Sharma calls "temporal laborers," whose time matters only as it can be enlisted into supporting the productive and reproductive goals of others. "As the expendable bodies of a labor force that can easily be replenished," Sharma observes, "there is no need for the structures of capital to endow [service workers'] time with importance. Biopower rears its head through divestment as well as regulation" (2014, 56). Biopolitical divestment and the devaluing of the time of these (racialized, classed, and gendered) segments of the labor force are also reflected in current federal policy, in which temporal governance primarily appears not in the form of regulatory safeguards but in the lack of protections afforded to low-wage workers. The drive to maximize profit by containing labor costs means that most service employers no longer provide the reliable number of work hours that made American factory work of the mid-twentieth century a relatively dependable source of (male) family wages. Yet despite these dramatic transformations in the temporal structure of low-wage work, federal labor laws are largely unchanged from their first writing in the 1930s era of the New Deal, focusing on the protection of workers from the abuses of *over*work rather than the contemporary problems of *under*employment, insufficient hours, and schedule instability (Boushey 2016).

The failure to pass federal legislation that would more substantively protect the time of low-wage workers reveals how states have become, as Angela Stuesse observes, "the principal enforcers of neoliberalism, wielding regulatory powers in ways that ensure that capitalist logic can govern society" (2016, 9). In the absence of robust protections, workers' time and labor are bent to the demands of neoliberal capital, acutely attuned to the hour-by-hour shifts in corporate need and consumer demand. Technological developments, from remote monitoring to scheduling software, have in turn allowed employers ever greater power over employees' labor time and activity. The computer modeling programs that predict the ebb and flow of customers across a working day allow managers to break down customer flow to increments as small as fifteen minutes and schedule workers only for times when they are expected to be needed. In some cases, this might mean assigning employees to mere four-hour shifts that will not even cover their transportation and childcare expenses. Nadia Smith, a US-born mother of two currently employed in food service, told me that she had left her previous job as a supermarket cashier because the inadequate hours did not cover the cost of subway transportation and childcare on the days that she was scheduled to work. "In my other job," she recalled, "I wasn't really getting no hours or nothing like that. And it was a waste of time. I'm like, I'm just spending money to come to work and basically you're not having nothing [no hours] for me."

In this convergence of neoliberal forms of state and corporate temporal governance, it is individuals and families, rather than governments and corporations, who take on the risks associated with fluctuating income and insufficient hours (Butler 2004; Hacker 2006; Stuesse 2016). Some of the women with whom I spoke described searching for "hours" as like a second unpaid job as they perused online company bulletin boards advertising available shifts, called other store locations that might need last-minute replacements, or volunteered themselves as substitutes on home health care cases. In an example of what Guy Standing (2014) has called "working to work," referring to the amount of unpaid time and labor that a precariously employed workforce spends looking for and securing paid employment, this often meant spending money and unremunerated time traveling between cases or other jobs to cobble together enough to cover their economic needs. For example, Cintia Baron, a home health worker turned union organizer whom we will meet again in the final chapter, recalled vividly to me the many hours spent on New York's buses and subways to reach far-flung cases and the exhaustion of coming home after a twelve-hour day in which only seven hours might be considered "on the clock."

Control over the structure and amount of labor time, or what women called "hours," is thus one mechanism through which service employers make workers' time both available and disposable. Despite job advertisements that promise flexibility for employees, those seeking jobs in the service sector quickly learn that limiting their hours of availability decreases both their chances of being hired and, once hired, the number of hours that they are scheduled to work (Henly, Shaefer, and Waxman 2006; Lambert 2008; Ray 2018). The clear message is that the most desirable worker is the one who is willing to make herself completely open to labor. Corporate practices of intentional underemployment also increase pressure on workers to accept otherwise undesirable working hours and conditions. Although primarily a strategy to avoid company responsibility for employee benefits and overtime, chronic underemployment also produces a sense of labor hours as a scarce resource that must be prioritized over family outings, schooling, prenatal care, and other claims to workers' time (Ray 2018).

Other mechanisms through which corporations exercise temporal control over workers include practices of surveillance and auditing designed to ensure punctuality and adherence to desired schedules (A Better Balance 2020; Guendelsberger 2019; Mankekar and Gupta 2019). A number of the women I interviewed described policies modeled on contemporary credit and banking systems: employees accrue credit, or "points," through actions such as arriving early or by staying after the nominal end of a scheduled shift. They can also lose credit by calling out or through other infractions of company policy, and employees whose credit drops below a certain threshold can be fired. Mary-Ann Joseph, whose narrative began this book, explained that she would "choose" to miss or delay prenatal care if she discovered that her weekly schedule conflicted with her medical appointment. "I would have to go to work," she said.

> Push the appointment to a further date or whatever. I couldn't just come late to my shift, not without a demerit. I would need to make sure that someone was there to cover me, and I would have to give up the whole shift. At [this department store], you lose credits if you call out: one credit for a weekday, two credits for a weekend. I just started there so I haven't had an opportunity to build credit, and if you go too low they let you go. My work is not very flexible that way.

Through such forms of temporal governance, those employees who can "invest" additional unpaid time in the company are rewarded with credits that cushion them against future uncertainties. Those who are unable to do so are made more economically and temporally precarious; with few resources to navigate conflicts between labor time and other commitments, they find that any call-outs, regardless of the reason, put them at risk of losing their jobs (Williams 2006).

In both policy and practice, corporate regulations governing lateness and absences thus reiterate the power of employers over workers' time, even when it comes at the expense of their (reproductive) health and well-being. This was brought home when I spoke to Sabrina Georges at Beaumont Hospital. Twenty years old and expecting her first child, she worked as an expeditor in the shoe department of a national chain store, bringing shoes from the stockroom to salespeople on the floor and cleaning up discarded items after customers had rejected them. During her training, she told me, her supervisor had described the company's absence policy as "three strikes and you're out." Each unexcused call-out would result in a demerit, and employees were subject to termination after accruing three demerits. Her round face creasing with displeasure, Sabrina bitterly described how her manager had applied these punitive absence policies even when she thought that she was going into preterm labor:

> I'll give you an example. When I was at work, I had to come to the hospital because I wasn't feeling well. My back was hurting, my lower back. I was having contractions; I was having the Braxton-Hicks [contractions; also known as "false labor"]. They [at the emergency room] was like, "I'm glad that you did come in." I brung the letter [from the emergency room physicians] to my job, and my supervisor denied it. So I wound up getting points [demerits] because of it, so that's one strike.

Blurring the line between labor and the penal system, corporate "three strike" policies directly reference the punitive sentencing laws that, in many states, require mandatory sentence lengths for individuals convicted of their third felony (including for nonviolent drug offenses). Critics have denounced the highly unequal consequences of these laws, pointing out that Black and brown people are disproportionately likely to be subject to police surveillance and therefore to be arrested and incarcerated under "three strike" laws. Further, they point out that mandatory sentences eliminate judges' ability to take mitigating circumstances or individual character into account. Echoing these critiques, the women I interviewed often complained that workplace absence policies did not distinguish between "good" workers, who used call-outs rarely and only in emergencies, and presumptively "bad" workers, who abused employer leniency. Further, they pointed out that corporate attendance policies failed to make exceptions even for reasonable medical causes—a widespread and well-documented problem (A Better Balance 2020). Sabrina's case is instructive, since Braxton-Hicks contractions can be distinguished from the onset of true labor only by the fact that contractions gradually subside rather than intensifying. Given the well-documented and complex problem of higher rates of preterm labor among Black women in the United States in general (D. Davis 2019; Krieger et al. 2018; March of Dimes 2020), I often heard providers at Beaumont encourage patients to come to the emergency room for a checkup if they had any warning signs of impending labor. Thus, Sabrina, already anxious about the effect of her physically demanding job on her pregnancy, was being a "good patient" and following medical advice when she decided to go to the hospital for evaluation rather than continuing her shift. The consequence, however, was a black mark on her employment record and the further reduction of her resources for navigating any future temporal conflicts.

As Sabrina suggests, supervisors were usually the targets of women's ire when they denied requests to change schedules or to excuse a call-out. In some cases, particularly in smaller businesses, it is possible that supervisors did have the power to provide these temporal accommodations and simply chose not to do so. Yet in other instances, supervisors were themselves subject to corporate surveillance and temporal governance and had little power to alter policies set by others. In large chain stores with elaborate work hierarchies, workplace policies are set at the national level; lower-level supervisors and floor managers, who often make only a dollar or two per hour more than the workers they manage, are monitored by higher-ranking supervisors or regional managers and have little discretion to alter schedules or make exceptions to company absence policies without incurring their own penalties. However, women often tended to see supervisors as the primary decision makers rather than as an instrument of larger entities in whose structures they occupied a relatively low place. In doing so, they ignored the levels of power that constrained supervisors as well as those whom they supervised.

Although I did not interview employers about their rationales for workplace policy, the importation of language from the criminal "justice" system into corporate temporal governance is not spurious, particularly in a context in which low-wage service workers, disproportionately women, generally come from the same communities where Black and brown men are most endangered by "three strike" laws. Scholars have shown how low-wage service and care labor (for women) and mass incarceration (for men) rose as parallel and interlinked processes, offering a "fix" to large-scale and destabilizing economic shifts by "channeling public expenditure and state power in the management of surplus population, generating employment, profits, and social stability" (Winant 2021, 18; see also Wacquant 2009). In the "afterlife of slavery" (Hartman 2007), racialized bodily and spatio-temporal discipline is experienced both inside and outside the workplace. Whether through mass incarceration or exploitative labor practices, Black and brown communities are too often "robbed" of time (Coates 2015; B. Cooper 2017).

"I Control My Time"

Given the rigid and often punitive nature of temporal governance in many service workplaces, I was taken aback by some women's assertion that they, and not their employers, "controlled" their time. One chilly winter afternoon, I interviewed Jasmine Tremain, a vivacious US-born twenty-one-year-old in her first pregnancy. At the time of our interview, she was such a recent hire at a high-volume fashion retail chain that she was still carrying around the company's regulations and policies manual, which she consulted at various times as we spoke. Like that of most retail workers in my research, Jasmine's schedule changed from week to week and was posted only one week in advance. If she found out that her shift conflicted with her prenatal care appointment, she would advertise her shift on her company's online message board and hope that someone picked it up. Her workplace permitted workers three excused call-outs provided that they supplied a doctor's note stating the reason for their absence (a common and detested form of temporal governance that forces workers to expend time, money, and energy attending medical appointments even if they are only suffering from a bad cold). Employees who exceeded this number, even for documented medical reasons, could be subject to termination, and Jasmine was very aware that she might need to use her allowable call-outs later in her pregnancy. Whether she was able to find a co-worker willing to take her shift or was forced to call out, the temporal conflict between work and prenatal care would result in the loss of a day's income.

Yet despite what I perceived as unforgiving labor policy, Jasmine insisted to me, "I control my own time." Seeing my confusion, she quickly elaborated, "As long as I can find someone to work [in] my place, my supervisor doesn't care. It's just me that loses the money. So, I control my time." Similarly, Jerusha Smith, a twenty-three-year-old Jamaican home health aide pregnant with her first child, told me, "I do feel that I can control my time. All I do is call the [home care] agency and let them know that I have an appointment to go to the doctor, and they will send somebody [else] in [to work instead]. But they will probably ask for proof that I went to the doctor." For Karl Marx and later observers of the Industrial Revolution and its aftermath, the labor practices that made workers interchangeable and replaceable cogs in the factory line stripped them of autonomy over their bodies and identification with their labor products. In the service industry of the late twentieth and early twenty-first centuries, this alienation from the work process and product has arguably become so normalized that employees' recognition of their interchangeability can in fact provide them a sense of control over their conditions of labor. Aware that their supervisors' only concern was that sufficient bodies were available to work, Jasmine and Jerusha felt free to call out, provided that someone else could work in their place.

In various ways, the women I spoke with thus resisted the impositions of corporate temporal governance on their time and person. Yet this autonomy is severely constrained since, in giving up a shift to attend a prenatal appointment, Jasmine and Jerusha essentially sustain financial penalties as a result of their decision to prioritize care. As Benjamin Snyder (2016, 183) points out, the realities of survival in a deregulated market encourage workers to see themselves as "entrepreneurs" of their own time. In an example of Marx's "double freedom" ([1867] 2019) of the wage worker, they are "free" to work harder and faster in the hope of getting ahead. They are also, however, "free" of any source of social support other than their wages. By framing the forced decision to *either* work to earn money *or* seek prenatal care as a choice that reflects their individual control over their time, they naturalize and render unremarkable the forms of temporal governance that shape low-wage service work and reproduce hierarchies of race, gender, and class.

Protecting Time: State and Local Policy and Entrenched Inequalities

Despite the ever-increasing prominence of low-wage hourly service workers as a share of the labor force, policy makers have been slow, or reluctant, to respond to these new temporal landscapes of work. In recent years, however, there has been increasing public and policy recognition of the negative effects of temporal precarity on workers, as well as the ways in which temporal exploitation intersects with broader social and economic inequalities (Boushey 2016; Kalleberg 2009). Mobilization around the protection of workers' time—an early pillar of union organizing—has again become the center of labor and social activism. However, most of the legislative successes have been achieved at the level of individual cities and states, reflecting a deeply polarized national context in which many federal lawmakers are reluctant to support legislation that might be seen as "interfering" in the "private" space of business.

As noted earlier, when I began my research in 2014, New York City had just implemented the Pregnant Workers Fairness Act (PWFA) and the Paid Safe and Sick Leave Act. These pieces of legislation were an important step forward from the 1978 federal Pregnancy Discrimination Act, with its difficult burden of proof that required pregnant workers to show that they were treated differently than non-pregnant workers with "similar disabilities." They also represented significant successes in an American labor environment with scarce protections for low-wage service workers, for whom the consequences of lost wages can be dramatic and tragic. Analyses of household savings in 2016, when I was carrying out my interviews, showed that 63 percent of Americans had less than five hundred dollars to fall back on in the event of an unexpected expense (McGrath 2016). In such households, any reduction in income can send families into chaos, entailing decisions about where to borrow and where to cut to meet pressing expenses. Nyanna Jones, a twenty-four-year-old employee at a national retail chain pregnant with her first child, told me, "I work hard but when I don't get my whole paycheck, I have to make decisions. I always pay my Metrocard to get to work, and my water, maybe electric, my rent and my phone, but maybe I don't pay my cable that month or something." According to the National Low Income Housing Coalition, there is not a single state in America where a full-time minimum-wage worker can rent a one-bedroom apartment for less than 30 percent of their income—the definition of "affordable housing"—and more than 11 million households spend more than half of their income on rent (Appelbaum 2016). For financially precarious low-wage workers, the loss of a job or long-term reduction of hours can lead to eviction and even homelessness (Boushey 2016; Coe 2019). This is particularly true in New York City, where the cost of living is among the highest in the United States.

Yet, however significant, these acts alone have limited power to reshape low-wage workers' vulnerability. Forty hours of paid sick leave, the maximum that companies with fewer than a hundred employees must provide under New York's Paid Safe and Sick Leave Act, may be adequate for a salaried worker who can use one or two of their paid sick hours to attend prenatal care at the beginning or end of their workday. However, this model fits poorly with the temporal regimes of low-wage service work, where women are usually required to call out of an entire shift to attend prenatal care rather than simply arriving late or leaving early. If paid sick leave is used to cover a seven- or eight-hour shift, a pregnant service worker who must attend monthly or even weekly medical appointments will quickly exhaust forty hours of annual paid sick leave. Further, these hours accrue slowly (at the rate of one hour per thirty hours worked, rather than being provided up front) and cannot be transferred between employers. Given the high employee turnover in the low-wage service industry (Boushey 2016), many workers may leave their jobs before they reach the maximum number of allowable paid sick hours.

While the women I interviewed universally expressed support for these acts, they also made clear that they did not address what was, for most, the most salient factor shaping the reproductive temporalities of low-wage families and households: the (lack of) availability of paid leave to support themselves after the birth of their child. The United States is notoriously one of only four countries, along with Swaziland, Lesotho, and Papua New Guinea, and the only industrialized nation in the world that does not guarantee some paid leave after the birth of a child. Indeed, the absence of paid family leave and other family-friendly policies is considered a primary reason why the number of American women in the paid workforce has stalled, contrary to the trend in other countries, affecting both familial and national budgets (Miller and Tankersley 2019). To give but a sampling of other national policies, Pakistan guarantees at least twelve weeks of paid leave, the United Kingdom provides thirty-nine weeks, Japan offers fifty-two weeks, and Estonia guarantees over eighty weeks of paid parental leave. Sweden and Norway provide over a year of paid leave for new parents (Francis, Cheung, and Berger 2021).

In the United States, only one federal policy exists: the 1993 Family and Medical Leave Act (FMLA). Intended to represent just the first step toward a more family-friendly work environment, it stands some thirty years later as the most significant legislation for workers who need time off to care for themselves or dependents. Polls show that about 80 percent of Americans say that they support paid family leave (Miller and Tankersley 2019). However, most federal lawmakers have declined to consider legislating paid leave or raising taxes to pay for them, arguing that such mandates are a burden on small businesses and that these decisions are best negotiated between individual employers and their employees (Barrón-López and Liebelson 2015). As of 2018, fewer than 40 percent of all medium to large companies provided any paid family leave, and small businesses were even less likely to offer these kinds of benefits. Those businesses that do provide paid family leave disproportionately employ "professional" workers; tech giants such as Google, Facebook, Yahoo, and Netflix, for example, have garnered much press for their paid parental leave policies. Against the objection that paid family leave is bad for their bottom line, these companies argue that it makes them more able to recruit and retain valuable skilled workers. Such formal recognition of workers' value is rarely extended to the low-wage service sector, despite a growing recognition of the cost to companies of replacing experienced workers (Boushey and Glynn 2012).

For many working people, the FMLA is thus the sole policy protecting their time to care for themselves and others. Yet the FMLA guarantees only up to twelve weeks of *unpaid* leave in a twelve-month period and applies only to workers employed for more than a year at a company of more than fifty people. Nationally, only 56 percent of American workers are covered by the FMLA, and Black and brown workers are disproportionately likely to be ineligible. Forty-eight percent of Latinx workers, 47 percent of Asian American workers, and 43 percent of Black workers work in jobs that do not qualify them for protected time under the FMLA (A Better Balance 2022). At Beaumont Hospital, after the twice-weekly informational and recruitment sessions during which I presented information about the Pregnant Workers Fairness Act, the Paid Safe and Sick Leave Act, and the FMLA, waiting patients frequently asked me whether they would qualify for postpartum leave under the FMLA. However, it quickly became clear that most were ineligible either because they had worked at their company for fewer than twelve months or because their company employed fewer than fifty workers, a typical situation among many of the mom-and-pop retail and food stores in the area. Moreover, while the FMLA provides job security for eligible workers, it offers no protection against financial precarity. As Cintia Baron, the union organizer, recalled of her previous employment as a home health aide, "The weeks that I had to pay the electric [bill] were tough ones. That's how tight the budget was. You think we can afford to not get paid for six weeks?" After our discussions, several women concluded that it would be preferable to be laid off since they would then become eligible for unemployment benefits. Given the frequent "churn" of low-wage workers between service jobs, they trusted that they would be able to find the same or a similar position once they decided to return to work.

But it is not only financial well-being that is at stake when pregnant or postpartum low-wage workers are forced out of work. Nyanna Jones, the employee at a national retail chain, told me that she hoped to take three or four months off after the birth of her child. Having just been promoted from the entry-level position, known as "white" level, to "yellow," the level immediately below a supervisory position, she was pleased at her rapid ascent and the small bump in hourly wages that it provided. The discovery of her pregnancy, however, had forced a difficult decision. Her company was willing to provide up to eight weeks of unpaid leave but would terminate her employment if she did not return to work after that point. Although she was confident that she would be rehired whenever she wished to return to work, company policy only allowed her to return as an entry-level associate, meaning that she would lose all the status and benefits that she had accrued through her promotion. Upon hearing about the FMLA, Nyanna hoped that it might provide a solution to her dilemma.

In the cluttered room where I conducted interviews, I recited the requirements of the FMLA and asked Nyanna to provide her expected due date and the date that she had been hired by her employer. We fell silent as we simultaneously realized that she would fall short of the twelve months of employment required for FMLA eligibility by just thirteen days. Nyanna's disappointment was plain on her face as she explained to me,

> It's my first [child], you know. And I want to experience it all. I just feel like I won't be ready [to return after eight weeks of leave]. . . . But I really don't want to start again [as an entry-level employee]. It's not only being promoted and more money. For me, it's the fact that, your skill is being recognized and, you know, the respect. To say, "Okay. You came in

as white [entry-level]. Now this is where you're at now." But I guess as a mom, you have to make sacrifices, you know?

As she makes clear, it is not only the loss of income that makes the prospect of starting over as an entry-level associate so distressing. Perhaps even more important to her is the negative effect of such forced starting-over on her self-perception as a valued professional ascending a career ladder. Yet, like Jasmine and Jerusha, who saw their "choice" to give up a shift to attend prenatal care as evidence of their control over time, Nyanna interprets her dilemma within an individual rather than a structural framework, enlisting a familiar gendered narrative of maternal sacrifice to justify the failures of both states and corporations to value and protect her reproductive time. In this explanatory framework, choosing between professional mobility and caring for an infant becomes an apparently inevitable condition of (good) motherhood rather than an injustice produced through indifferent social and political structures.

Nyanna's experience reveals how state and corporate temporal governance shape reproductive temporalities by forcing low-wage workers to choose between returning to work far earlier than they are emotionally or physically ready—sometimes within two weeks of giving birth (Paquette 2015)—and accepting the financial and professional consequences of giving up their jobs. Such constrained choices have both health and economic effects. Research shows that women with short or no leaves after birth are at higher risk of postpartum depression than those with twelve weeks or longer (Kornfeind and Sipsma 2018). Paid leave for new parents has also been found to promote breastfeeding and parental bonding, with important mental and physical benefits for both parents and infant (Mirkovic, Perrine, and Scanlon 2016; Pihl and Basso 2019). Further, when workers leave jobs rather than return earlier than they would like, it costs them benefits and promotions accrued on the job and reinforces common perceptions of low-wage service workers as low-skill and easily replaceable.

Failures of policy with respect to time thus amplify conditions of stratified reproduction across axes of class, race/ethnicity, gender, and sexuality, among others. Indeed, these durable inequalities are embedded in the writing of the FMLA, since workers' ability to use this policy to their benefit fundamentally depends on their household's ability to survive for an extended period on a reduced (or no) income. As might be expected, economic stresses on low-income families are exacerbated by the loss of labor time during the pregnancy: pregnant workers in hourly-wage jobs often report pay reductions in the months prior to birth due to fewer hours worked for pregnancy-related causes such as seeking prenatal care, which decreases the pool of savings necessary to contemplate unpaid leave (Ingraham 2018). One study of maternal leave policy found that in the period from 2006 to 2008, a full third of the participants who took unpaid leave reported that they had been forced to borrow money or use savings to cover their bills, and a further 15 percent had enrolled in public assistance in order to survive (Laughlin 2011).

The FMLA's class bias is thus evident in its baseline expectation that workers have sufficient savings to carry them through this period or that they are in dual-income relationships where the remaining income is sufficient to sustain the household. Given the well-documented disparity between male and female incomes, this reveals the rootedness of the FMLA in a traditional familial model: a heterosexual middle-class household with a male breadwinner. Although women earn less than men across all racial and ethnic groups, studies show a relatively limited differential between the earnings of white women and those of women of color. Racial differences in household income are produced almost exclusively by *male* income disparities, since Black and brown men tend both to be employed in less lucrative professions than white men and to be compensated less than their white counterparts in the same positions (Badger et al. 2018). Race-based income inequalities in turn mean that the families of (heterosexual) Black and brown men have fewer economic resources to survive an extended reduction in household income.

The situation for female-headed or same-sex female households, in which both partners earn "female" wages, can be even more dire; while the median dual-income family's earnings drop by about 10 percent following the birth of a child, the income of single mothers drops by 42 percent (Ingraham 2018).

The FMLA thus perpetuates entrenched raced, gendered, and classed ideologies about the value of different people's time, as well as the ends to which their time and labor should be "properly" directed. Despite demographic shifts in both the full-time labor force and family formation, the (white) middle-class "stay-at-home mom" made possible by the gendered, classed, and racial privilege of a male breadwinner continues to be culturally valorized. This is not to say that middle-class families have all the needed supports; the limited availability of paid parental leave, flex-work policies, and high-quality affordable daycare, especially compared with other industrialized countries, undoubtedly contributes to findings that parents in the United States spend more money and are more likely to report unhappiness than parents in other countries (Dell'Antonia 2016). Given cultural values around independence and individualism, parents are more likely to blame their own failures rather than those of the state when it turns out that they cannot do it all and still remain economically, emotionally, and physically solvent.

Yet this burden falls far more heavily on low-income women and families who do not have the economic resources to make the (always constrained) choices available to better-off households. Thus, although professional women also face pregnancy discrimination and conflicts between labor and gestational time (e.g., Kitroeff and Silver-Greenberg 2019), their experiences stand in stark contrast to the ambivalence toward the reproductive time of low-income women, particularly those of color, as we will consider in more detail in the next chapter. For this latter group, their work in caring for their own children and households, as opposed to their paid work supporting the reproductive needs of wealthier families, continues to be seen as less deserving of either moral or economic support (Barnes 2015; Briggs 2017; Roberts 1997; Ross and Solinger 2017).

Given the few and sparse corporate or state protections of their reproductive time during either pregnancy or the postpartum period, most of the women I spoke with thus echoed the words of Jerusha Smith, the home health aide, who told me emphatically, "The only time I get paid is when I clock in."

"We're Not Gonna Worry about Those Jobs": Theories of Ethnic Succession and the Refusal of Reform

Despite local successes such as the Pregnant Workers Fairness Act and the Paid Safe and Sick Leave Act, entrenched social and racial hierarchies continue to inform a widespread reluctance to push for workplace temporal reform. One afternoon, I talked with Angela Mason, a policy analyst at a New York City advocacy organization serving home health aides and other direct care workers. She observed, "People look at these jobs that are typically minimum-wage jobs, whether they are at McDonald's or in homecare or whatever, as temporary or insignificant. They're like, 'We're not gonna worry about those jobs. Hopefully people will get out of those jobs. They'll go to college, or they'll . . .'" She trailed off in thought, and then resumed with indignation,

> It's ignoring the fact that those jobs are permanent for a lot of people. That's where they will work. When new immigrant groups come in, they often fill homecare jobs because it's a job that's more accessible to them than some other jobs. But the idea that we don't need to value that work because eventually you and yours will move out and be better than them, so don't worry—that premise is totally flawed.

For Angela, misguided theories of ethnic replacement underlie the lack of political and social will to transform the conditions of low-wage and precarious work. Occupying an outsized place in the myth of the American Dream, ethnic replacement posits a vision of history in which each successive group of ethnic migrants starts at the bottom of the social and economic ladder and, over generations of hard work and cultural assimilation, works itself into the middle class and beyond. Intimately entwined with the cultural valorization of self-reliance, this ideological trope serves to justify conditions of precarity and exploitation by asserting that suffering is a temporary, even necessary, condition that every migrant group must endure before moving up the ethno-economic ladder. In this national mythology, the ability of some ethnic groups to enter middle-class America justifies the current and future exploitation of others.

Theories of ethnic replacement are thus fundamentally stories about time, reflecting the supreme twentieth-century confidence that every generation will live better than the last. Yet, as Angela points out, this teleology depends on a collective bad faith, a term coined by philosopher Jean-Paul Sartre and repurposed by anthropologists to describe strategies of deliberate self-deception that allow individuals and collectivities to avoid acknowledging complicity with systems of structural violence (Holmes 2013; Scheper-Hughes 1993). The continuing popular investment in theories of ethnic replacement ignores the fact that the opportunities for advancement in the twenty-first century are very different from those that were possible in the previous century, as well as the ways in which the legacy of race and racism shapes the American social landscape. In the mid-twentieth century, the entry of a generation of Jewish, Irish, and Italian immigrants, previously seen as ethnic Others, into the (white) middle class was facilitated by a suite of political and economic benefits enjoyed by the post–World War II generation (Brodkin Sacks 1998). Immigrants today, more likely to come from countries in Africa, the Caribbean, Latin America, and Asia than from Europe, face racist ideologies and hierarchies that continue to mark them as Other regardless of their class status. At the same time, they are migrating during a period of neoliberal expansion, with far fewer policies and programs to support low-income people.

A free employment newspaper distributed around Brooklyn showing the number of advertisements for home health aides. Photograph by the author.

Such historical and generational shifts are not lost on immigrants themselves. One day, I sat with Ms. Hernández, a receptionist at Beaumont Hospital's clinic, as she scheduled a first prenatal appointment with a heavily pregnant woman who had just arrived from Jamaica. After the woman left the counter to find a seat in the crowded waiting room, Ms. Hernández turned to me and remarked sadly, "When I came from Guyana, I could get a job, save for a house. I'm not sure why they come now. It is so hard to make a living." Suffering the "conjugated oppression" (Bourgois 1988) of multiple axes of inequality, today's low-wage workers occupy a labor landscape that offers few opportunities for class mobility.

Conclusion

As we have seen, low-wage service workers are subject to forms of corporate and state temporal governance that make them vulnerable to both economic and temporal precarity. Corporate practices of (under)scheduling and temporal surveillance pressure women to make themselves constantly available to labor, while the limited protections available to them either through the workplace or through the state underscore the lack of value accorded to their time to care for themselves and for others. The harms inflicted by exploitative forms of temporal governance are not restricted to workers; research suggests that the children of parents with nonstandard and unpredictable work schedules also experience deleterious effects due to household economic insecurity, diminished time for parental investment, and maternal stress, particularly in the first year of life (Li et al. 2014; Schneider and Harknett 2022). By constraining the reproductive temporalities of low-income individuals and families, the temporal regimes of service work thus perpetuate entrenched gendered, classed, and racial inequalities across the generations.

For pregnant workers, navigating the temporal regimes of service workplaces can be even more fraught since, in many cases, they are expected to maintain the tempo of labor while adding prenatal care to an often delicate balancing act. In the following chapter, we will examine the intersection of labor, clinical, and gestational time to consider how the temporal regimes of labor and clinical settings shape pregnant service workers' experiences of working and accessing prenatal care.

2

Working While Pregnant

Conflicts between Labor, Clinical, and Gestational Time

Michaela Johnson was becoming visibly upset as she related the circumstances that led to her leaving her previous job just a couple of weeks before we spoke at Beaumont Hospital. She had been working at a discount retail store on a busy commercial avenue for about a year when she became pregnant with her first child. Even through her excitement, she could tell that her managers were none too happy about the news. It was a small store, and the managers relied on her to carry out much of the work without supervision: changing mannequins and displays, returning merchandise from the fitting rooms to the shop floor, lifting and unpacking boxes of clothes for display, helping customers, and working the register. She considered herself a hard worker and a valuable employee and thought that she would be able to manage.

Around her eighth week of pregnancy, Michaela's nausea worsened, exacerbated by the constant bending and lifting that many of her tasks required. On one particular occasion, she recalled, she had felt so unwell that she had to run to the store restroom to vomit. Still feeling dizzy and nauseated, she asked her supervisor whether she could go home for the day. By way of a response, her supervisor gestured around the floor, telling her that the store needed to be fully cleaned as "the company" (regional headquarters) was coming to inspect the following day. Michaela tossed her long black hair over her shoulder in a gesture of indignation as she recounted her disbelieving retort: "I just threw up. I don't feel good! How much cleaning do you expect me to do?"

After that incident, Michaela asked her managers whether they could put her exclusively on register duty until her morning sickness subsided.

"Because," she told me, "I had no problem when I worked at the register all day. I could make it through the whole day." Her managers, however, refused to countenance her requests for accommodation, even on the hottest summer days when the central air failed to circulate and the floor staff surreptitiously fanned themselves with newspapers when customers weren't watching. Michaela recalled, "They'd say, 'Oh well, you can do registering but I also need you to go lift these clothes over here too. We need to get these clothes out [to the shop floor]' or 'Those clothes are backed up, they need to be put away.'"

Shaking her head at the remembered injustice, Michaela continued,

> I'd say, "I need water, I need something to eat, I need to sit down for a few minutes." And they'd laugh. . . . It was like they didn't really take into consideration [that] "Here's this hard worker that we had, we know this is not her norm to just only want to do the register." But they didn't care. They don't care about your health; they care more about their store. But I'm not gonna have an unhealthy baby because they wanna be ignorant.

Michaela's experiences were not unique. I had first conceived this project as a study of the disarticulation between the temporal regimes of service labor and safety net prenatal care. Yet in the many conversations that followed, the women involved in my research described in vivid detail a different temporal arc—that of gestational time—and the physical toll of service work on pregnant bodies that were first sick and then increasingly heavy and cumbersome as the months progressed. Home health aides described lifting and caring for clients with limited or no mobility, while workers in food service recalled standing for hours amid the unpleasantness of food smells that they could not escape. Still others, employed in the demanding retail sector, endured long shifts during which they were required to remain on their feet even as their feet swelled in their shoes and their backs ached from the added weight of their expanding bellies.

Their stories were a constant reminder of the crucial importance of thinking not only about reproductive labor, but also about laboring reproductive bodies. Following their lead, this chapter examines how the deeply racialized "demands, logics, and temporalities" (Mankekar and Gupta 2019, 425) of service work are refracted in and through workers' pregnant bodies as they try to synchronize the pace of labor to the arc of gestational time. Building on the previous chapter's concerns with temporal precarity and temporal governance, we will see how the labor time of different types of service work shaped women's capacity to routinely schedule and attend prenatal care at Beaumont, where the volume of patients often made rescheduling timely appointments an impossibility. In some cases, pregnant workers' ability to reconcile the conflicts between labor, gestational, and clinical time was enabled by supportive relationships with supervisors and co-workers. In others, participants described supervisors who expected their pregnant employees to maintain the unflagging tempo of service work, often insinuating that their slower, fatigued, and heavy bodies were "out of sync" with the time discipline of ideal workers. In their adherence (or lack thereof) to the formal articulations of corporate and state temporal governance, supervisors thus played a key role in producing the temporal regimes of specific workplaces. As we will see, workers' relationships with supervisors and co-workers profoundly shaped their ability to navigate the often discrepant temporalities of working and pregnancy.

Labor Time, Gestational Time: Work and Pregnancy

In the anthropology of reproduction, a small but important body of work has focused on the intersection between pregnancy and work. Much of this research focuses on new reproductive arrangements, such as surrogacy and gamete donation, which problematize traditional definitions of "work time." Pregnant surrogates who must monitor what they eat and drink, curtail sexual activity, attune themselves to expected movements of the fetal body, take medications, and attend medical appointments are, in a very real sense, always working (Deomampo 2016; Pande 2014; Ragoné 1994). As Melinda Cooper and Catherine Waldby argue, surrogacy and gamete donation involve the extraction of work through the body's "*in vivo* temporalities"—"the temporalities of ingestion, metabolism, endocrine cycles, excretion, and parturition" (2014, 227)—that cannot be partitioned into industrial clock time. In the case of an egg donor, value, as measured by the extraction of numerous "good-quality" egg cells, is produced through the metabolic and reproductive activity of the donor's body that exceeds concepts of a temporally delimited workday. Such "clinical labor" (Cooper and Waldby 2014) challenges the supposedly clearly demarcated distinctions between "labor time" and time "off the clock."

Fewer anthropological studies have focused explicitly on experiences of working and pregnancy for women who are not participating in these new reproductive arrangements. As a form of labor, service sector work incorporates much of the "time discipline" (Thompson 1967) that emerged during England's Industrial Revolution, albeit in a very different political-economic and cultural moment. In his classic essay, E. P. Thompson describes how industrialization ushered in a historically unprecedented change in human labor activity and forms of temporal surveillance, which he calls "time discipline." In the prior agrarian society, work rhythms had been organized by seasonal and circadian rhythms. Decisions about the timing, pace, and duration of labor were made by individuals and collectivities according to the tasks that needed to be completed, and patterns of work often involved periods of heightened activity (for example, during fall harvest) followed by long periods of rest (during the winter months). With the Industrial Revolution, these rhythms largely gave way to the highly regimented "clock time" that governed factory shift work. Clock-based time discipline became the central tenet of Taylorist scientific management, named after American Frederick Winslow Taylor, who in the late nineteenth century introduced novel methods for extracting often punishing levels of productivity and efficiency from factory laborers. In this new era, workdays were divided into sharply demarcated and strictly monitored periods of labor and rest. Tasks were deskilled, repetitive, and monotonous. Under constant surveillance, workers lost control over the tempo and timing of their work, expected to subordinate their own bodily rhythms to the clock time that dictated the pace and duration of work, rest, and the satisfaction of other needs, such as eating and sleeping. In sharp contrast to the past, the completion of a task did not signal the cessation of labor; it was only when a shift ended that a period of rest began, after which brief respite the workday would begin again. Obedience to factory clock time became the mark of the ideal laborer.

Other historians have traced the roots of time discipline to slavery and the emergence of racial capitalism, as managers on Caribbean sugar plantations monitored and meticulously documented the daily, and even hourly, productivity of enslaved people (Rosenthal 2018). Seen from this viewpoint, the temporal governance of service sector work is also part of the "afterlife of slavery" (Hartman 2007). Whether traced to exploitative labor in factories or on plantations, practices of capitalist time discipline introduced historically novel ways of conceptualizing, valuing, and monitoring time that structure contemporary service labor. Shift work requires that workers subsume their *in vivo* time—their own bodily rhythms—to accord with clock time; lunch and rest breaks are scheduled at regular intervals with little concern for the worker's actual experiences of hunger or fatigue, and in many workplaces, the frequency and length of bathroom breaks are similarly regulated. Jasmine Tremain, the new employee of a fashion retail store to whom we were introduced in the previous chapter, described the constant hunger and fatigue that plagued her throughout her shift:

> Because I'm on the [shop] floor, I can't eat when I want to. I do get a one-hour lunch and a fifteen-minute break, and I just try to eat as much as I can then to try to get through. Otherwise I'm just feeling nauseous and dizzy. Or I can take the 200 [code for a bathroom break] if I really need to sit down a minute. But I can't be doing that all the time, because they count them. That's hard, you know. I'm usually energetic, but now I'm

downbeat. I move slow, I lose breath really fast. But I'm just trying to not stress out and be happy, you know, for the baby.

The fantasy of the disciplined worker whose bodily functions are synchronized to the relentless tempo of capitalist labor is, of course, an illusion sustained through a refusal to acknowledge the changing corporeality of real bodies that get sick or injured, pregnant or aged. Medical anthropologists in the United States have documented similarly exploitative labor conditions in areas such as domestic work and the agricultural and meatpacking industries (Holmes 2013; Horton 2016; Rosenbaum 2017; Stuesse 2016). Yet pregnancy foregrounds the working body in highly visible and culturally resonant ways, serving as a powerful reminder of the violence of practices of time discipline that treat workers as well-regulated machines. Tasha Washington, a twenty-four-year-old originally from Guyana, for example, was working as a cashier in a fast-food restaurant when she became pregnant with her first child. Six months pregnant when I interviewed her at Beaumont Hospital, she pulled up her jeans to show me her ankles, still swollen from the previous day's shift. She explained,

> I went to work from 11:30 all the way to 9:00. I only had one break, thirty minutes. And my feet was hurting me so bad that I had to take them out of my sneakers. I'm basically standing up on the floor with my bare feet, and I got so angry [that] I asked if I could leave at 7:30. I don't mind you giving me the hours, but why would you give a pregnant person the hours of 11:30 all the way to 9:00? You could put a stool and I would sit and take orders all day, I won't mind. I'll work 12:00 to 12:00, you just let me sit down! . . . If I say [my feet] are swollen and I can't stand anymore, you as a manager should be understanding enough to be like, "Okay, take five. Sit down. Whenever you're ready, you can come and do it again."

Corporate practices of time and bodily discipline, particularly in sectors such as retail and fast food, thus produced profound disarticulations with gestational time, considered both as *in vivo* cyclical rhythms and the progression of pregnancy. Despite the Pregnant Workers Fairness Act, which mandates reasonable accommodations during pregnancy, women frequently reported supervisors who monitored the activities and tempo of their pregnant workers to ensure that they did not disrupt the meticulously regimented rhythms of work with unscheduled, too long, or too numerous bathroom or rest breaks. Similarly, if the physical or emotional changes of pregnancy cause employees to become "downbeat," as Jasmine puts it—to respond more slowly or expend more visible effort in responding to customers' or supervisors' requests—they may also be perceived as being "out of sync" with capitalist ideas of a desirable employee. As workers subordinated themselves to the temporal regimes and physical demands of service labor, their bodies swelled, slowed down, and became dizzy and nauseated. Pregnant bodies can thus be (re)shaped, injured, and weakened through their engagement with the time discipline of service work.

Longer-Term Conflicts between Labor and Gestational Time: Home Health Aides' Experiences

But not all service workers experience such direct forms of time discipline and surveillance. Among the home health aides who comprised more than one-third of my sample, the task-based work of washing dishes, bathing clients, and grocery shopping gave them more latitude to eat, use the bathroom, or sit down when they needed to, provided that their work was completed by the end of the shift. For them, the tensions produced by the discordance between labor and gestational time tended to take a longer arc, with conflicts becoming more apparent as their pregnancies progressed and clients questioned their ability to perform the assigned work to expected standards. Jayda Chamberlain, a twenty-two-year-old US-born home health aide pregnant with her first child, told me,

I was with him [her previous client] for ten hours a day. But they took me off the case, and they don't tell you really when you're gonna be taken off. It's kind of abrupt. [My supervisor] basically told me that the patient's family, or whatever, feels like it's too much work for me because I was pregnant.

Although she admitted that working for ten hours a day had been difficult at times, she declared, "At the end of the day, it was money, and I needed it." Her dissatisfaction with her supervisor's decision to remove her from her steady case was compounded by the fact that the "light" case that she was subsequently assigned was only four hours a day, three days a week. Moreover, where she was previously able to walk to her client's house, her new client lived an hour away by bus. Thus, in addition to the added expense of the necessity of purchasing a thirty-dollar weekly MetroCard (nearly an entire shift's wages), the time spent in commuting meant that the shift took up most of her working day even though it paid for only four hours of her time. This dramatic reduction in hours and earnings in turn had repercussions for future reproductive temporalities, particularly in her ability to take (unpaid) time with her child after the birth. Jayda pointed out, "It's only four hours a day, so it's not giving me a lot of money for me to be able to save. I contacted them and let them know, 'I'm having a child. I need hours, and for you to just take that away from me, it's hard.' But I don't know if they will do anything."

Other home health aides expressed their own concerns about their ability to fulfill required tasks as their pregnancies progressed, particularly in "hard" cases involving bedridden patients who needed to be lifted and moved frequently for bathing, feeding, and dressing. In a narrative that revealed her entangled anxieties about the changes of her pregnant body and the physical demands of her work, Lovelie St Jean, a twenty-six-year-old Haitian-born home health aide and single mother of one, described the worrisome exertion of trying to move her bedridden client, a man taller and heavier than she, in her seventh month of pregnancy. She wondered aloud to me, "If you're pregnant and trying to work, how you gonna deal with it? They [clients and/or supervisors] cannot deal with you no more because they have to find someone who has much more energy. So that's the worry every day . . . my body and my job." Underscoring the disjuncture between labor and gestational time, the pressure on Lovelie to maintain her previous pace and "energy" means striking a fraught balance between satisfying the expectations of her job—which, as a single mother, she desperately needed—and safeguarding her health and pregnancy. Yet requesting a "lighter" case during her pregnancy, as a few of the women I interviewed had done, did not necessarily resolve her dilemma. When I asked Lovelie whether she could ask to be transferred to a less demanding case, she replied simply, "I know the people [supervisors] already. If they change me, I'm not gonna go home with nothing, probably nothing until after the baby."

Lovelie's fear that she would not be reassigned to another case if she requested removal from her current client was shared by other home health aides. As Lovelie observes, agencies may simply tell pregnant aides that they have no suitable cases for them until after they give birth. Others pointed out that removal from a "hard" case did not necessarily mean an assignment to another of equivalent hours. It had been some time since I had seen Lucia Germaine, the thirty-five-year-old home health aide who had been removed from her steady case when her pregnancy was designated "high-risk." A few weeks after our first interview, Lucia and I met by happy accident as I was leaving Beaumont at the end of a long day. When I asked whether she had finally been assigned a steady case, she grimaced, telling me that her supervisor had agreed to assign her to "light" cases after receiving her papers from the hospital that cleared her to work. However, since "light" cases involve patients with less intensive care requirements, they also generally provide fewer hours, forcing aides to take sometimes considerable cuts to income or to string together multiple such cases. The latter was the situation for Lucia, who had been assigned to different morning and afternoon cases four days a week. "So now," Lucia concluded, "they've got me on the buses going all around town. It's nearly an hour between cases and I don't paid for that, and I come home exhausted. And guess what, I'm still pregnant!" As she underscores in her astute analysis, while supervisors may reassign pregnant workers to "light" cases ostensibly to protect their health, the reduction in labor hours may in fact increase their economic and physical stress. In this temporal accounting of labor, the considerable time and energy spent commuting in expectation of work are not considered worth paying for (Snyder 2016; Standing 2014).

As we have seen, in the logic of racial capital, Black and brown women's non-pregnant bodies appear eminently suitable for low-wage service work (e.g., Glenn 1992; Roberts 1997). Once they are pregnant, however, and by the same racist rationalization, the inability of their slower, larger, and sometimes sicker bodies to conform to the physical rigors and temporal regimes of service work undercuts their value as workers and makes them potentially "disposable." Michaela Johnson, the former retail worker turned call center worker, declared, "It's like you're not useful to the company because you're pregnant, because you move slow, and maybe you feel sick sometimes. . . . So they make it so you leave, and then they lose a good worker." Her reflection echoes the Marxist insight that capitalist production depends upon the extraction of energy, in the form of work, from those who have few other options to sustain themselves other than to sell their bodies in (low) wage labor. In their drive for profit, employers strive to wrest maximum "value" from a fixed number of paid labor hours by intensifying the pace of work (Marx [1867] 2019). When laboring bodies can no longer move at the tempo demanded of them, even for relatively short periods of time, they risk replacement with other laborers, seen as equally interchangeable and expendable. Given dominant perceptions of service work as low-status and unskilled labor (Boris and Parreñas 2010; Buch 2018), women who work in low-wage service sectors are particularly vulnerable to this particular form of racialized predatory capitalism.

Aspiring to a "Desk Job": Reproductive Risk, Ideologies of Motherhood, and Racialized Labor

In their negotiation of labor and gestational time, participants often expressed anxiety about the effects of service work's grueling forms of physical and time discipline on the health of their pregnancies. Several women confided that they had experienced at least one previous miscarriage, and many others worried that, despite the assurances of their doctors, the physical demands of service work might cause a reproductive loss. Ayesha Thomas, a twenty-seven-year-old Guyanese-born assistant manager at a fast-food restaurant and a mother of a seven-year-old, told me that she had recently suffered a miscarriage. At my expression of sympathy, she went on,

> That's OK. I'm getting over it now. This is like a back-to-back pregnancy because I got pregnant right after. So now, I'm always worried. Like, was eight hours working too much? Was [the miscarriage] because I'm on my feet all day? You know, they [the providers] were like, "No, that's not why," but of course, it's still in the back of your head. Every pain I feel, every pull I feel, I'm just like, "Oh, my God. What is that, you know?" And you're always checking for blood. My boyfriend is telling me—he says, "Stop. Will you stop?" But it's a constant worry, of course, because it's just what we do, as women and as mothers.

Gendered ideologies of "good" motherhood could thus be mobilized to various effects. In some cases, ideologies of motherhood served to justify otherwise undesirable working conditions. For example, Ayesha naturalized her reproductive anxieties about the physical demands of her job as part of the gendered labor of nurturance—"it's just what we do as women and as mothers"—while Jasmine, the retail employee, stated that she was trying not to "stress out" and "to be happy for the baby." Reflecting a widely held belief that pregnant people's emotional state can be felt by their fetuses, Jasmine articulated a (gendered) responsibility to care for her future child by moderating her negative emotions even as she naturalized the power of time discipline and rigid forms of temporal governance over her pregnant body. But in other cases, as we will explore later in this chapter, the women I spoke with pointed to their maternal responsibilities for the well-being of their future child to make claims upon employers for accommodations or to leave jobs that they felt jeopardized the health of their pregnancies.

Fears about work-related reproductive injury caused by frequent bending and lifting were also common. Sabrina Georges, the shoe expeditor of the previous chapter, told me,

> Everybody says, "You're pregnant, you shouldn't be carrying this stuff. You shouldn't do this. There should be something else that you can do." [The supervisors] can put me somewhere else, but [they say] "Oh, well, we don't have coverage so you'll have to go there [back to expediting]." . . . But if something happens to me while I'm pregnant, then they would be like, "Oh, we didn't know." But really, you did know. So now you're at risk at your job because they're not going to be like, "We're going to just let this go by."

As Sabrina points out, in refusing to acknowledge the risk to her reproductive well-being caused by their insistence on maintaining the uninterrupted pace of work, her supervisors are acting in bad faith—the false claim that one is unaware of one's implication in the reproduction of violence.

Concerns about the effects of routine aspects of service work on pregnant employees are not unfounded. As part of a larger focus on the travails of low-wage workers, the *New York Times* ran an investigative article that described the pregnancy losses of a number of women in low-wage positions after supervisors had denied their requests for light duty (Silver-Greenberg and Kitroeff 2018). Although the women I interviewed were more likely to cite long hours of standing and heavy lifting rather than nonstandard schedules as reproductive risks, there is evidence of higher risk for miscarriage, preterm birth, and low birth-weight for workers scheduled for nights or fluctuating shifts, likely due to changes in circadian rhythms as they are forced into shifting and atypical temporal regimes of labor (Bonde et al. 2013; Cai et al. 2019).

Such findings underscore the negative effects of the physical and temporal demands of service work on reproductive outcomes and well-being. Comparing service work to the relative privileges of middle-class professionals, several women spoke longingly of the relative ease of a "desk job." Nadia Smith, the US-born cashier at a fast-food restaurant with two small children, told me, "A lot of these females, they got it good, whoever's working at an office. They could just sit down all day." Echoing her sentiment, Clarice Taylor, pregnant with her second child and currently employed as a nanny for two young children, contrasted her current pregnancy with her previous experience as an accountant in her home country of Jamaica:

> Before, I was just sitting at a desk doing nothing. I loved it so much. Being pregnant and just sitting there doing your paperwork, it's way easier. But now that I'm doing the nanny thing, it's a struggle. . . . I'm pregnant and doing it all with the weight and the pains. The lower abdominal pains are terrible. It's hard.

In the context of service work, the relative ease of a desk job—which Clarice viewed as tantamount to "doing nothing"—was a frequently articulated aspiration. More than half of the participants told me that they intended to pursue their associate's (two-year) degrees at local community colleges or other vocational training in the hope of moving out of entry-level service sector positions. Improved pay was a primary consideration, although studies have shown that low-income workers often spend considerable time, money, and energy pursuing accreditation that may not lead to higher income (Ray 2018). However, a not-insignificant motivator was also the higher status attributed to work conducted while sitting down. Tasha Washington, the fast-food worker whose swollen feet and ankles bore witness to the long hours on her feet, told me, "I want to find a better job, somewhere that I could just sit down and work. A way better job than standing up, a different job from this."

Social scientists have long noted the relationship between social status and physical labor; manual "blue-collar" is typically seen as lower in status than "white-collar" work, which is typically conducted while sitting down. In his analysis of labor hierarchies on a farm in California, Seth Holmes (2013) distinguishes between managers, who spend most of the day sitting, the foremen and supervisors, who stand upright, and migrant fruit pickers, whose work requires long periods of stooping. Forms of labor map onto broader hierarchies of ethnicity and citizenship: managers, who were exclusively white or Asian American, were seen as civilized, clean, and educated—and thus "deserving" of the better-paid, less physical desk jobs. Meanwhile, foremen or supervisors, largely US-born Latinos who spoke English and enjoyed American citizenship, stood to supervise the migrant indigenous Triqui (Mexican) workers, who were dismissed as dirty, uneducated, and "naturally suited" to the hard labor of picking berries. This ethnic labor hierarchy, he argues, is one of the ways that structural violence becomes naturalized such that racialized bodies appear to "belong" in particular labor categories. Thus, higher-status, higher-paid seated work is considered to be white(ned) work, while stooping physical labor is synonymous with darker bodies.

These racialized hierarchies of labor and value are also evident in the predominantly female world of service sector work. Bodies made vulnerable through their position along multiple axes of race, gender, class, and citizenship—that is, low-resource, Black and brown, sometimes undocumented women—are expected to absorb labor conditions that would likely be considered unreasonable hardship if demanded of women in higher-status work, which is socially coded as white. As the narratives of Jasmine, Tasha, and Sabrina reveal, it is not uncommon for pregnant service sector workers to be denied requests for accommodation from heavy lifting or to be given shifts that require standing for hours with little time for relief (Bakst, Gedmark, and Brafman 2019; Silver-Greenberg and Kitroeff 2018).

Poster displayed at a 2016 New York City event to publicize the Pregnant Workers Fairness Act. Photograph by the author.

Such disparate treatment of pregnant bodies has a long and ignominious history in the United States. From the time of slavery, poor women, particularly those of color, have been forced through direct coercion or economic necessity to engage in arduous physical labor during pregnancy, leading to disproportionate rates of miscarriage, premature births, stillbirths, and maternal and infant death (D. Davis 2019; Mullings and Wali 2001; Roberts 1997; Ross and Solinger 2017). By contrast, the reproductive capacity of white(ned) women of higher social and economic status is often perceived as vulnerable, and they are protected from any perceived overexertion that might jeopardize their pregnancies. This is not to claim that pregnant women in professional occupations are immune from discriminatory practices; much research has clearly established that motherhood for middle- and upper-middle-class professional women negatively impacts career trajectories and earnings (Boushey 2016; McIntosh et al. 2012; Miller 2011; Williams 2001). Professional women, particularly those in male-dominated fields such as finance, often report being seen as irrational and uncommitted as they are systematically passed over for promotions and sidelined from important projects during their pregnancy. As one senior woman at one of the world's largest commodity trading companies put it to a *New York Times* reporter, "It was like they assumed my brain had totally changed overnight. I was seen as having no more potential" (Kitroeff and Silver-Greenberg 2019). Like service workers, professional working mothers often experience conflicts relating to scheduling inflexibility and lack of accommodations, albeit generally after the birth of their children rather than during pregnancy (e.g., Boushey 2016; Williams 2001).

Yet these different expressions of pregnancy discrimination starkly reveal how working women are differentially inserted into racialized labor regimes that posit the supposed physical endurance of darker female bodies as compared with white(ned) women's reproductive frailty. If pregnant (white) professional workers are assumed to be unmoored by their hormones and maternal instincts, becoming mentally and psychologically unfit for "rational" work, it is pregnancy's *physical* changes that make pregnant Black and brown workers potentially undesirable (service) workers. In "sitting down" labor, productivity tends not to be measured in the sharply differentiated and strictly policed division between "labor" and "rest" time typical of much service work; the rhythm of pregnant women's *in vivo* gestational time and the increased need to eat, sit, or urinate thus do not necessarily make them "bad workers." By contrast, the *in vivo* time of pregnant service workers and the pressing needs of their reproductive bodies for rest and sustenance threaten to disrupt the capitalist desire for a continuous and regulated rhythm of productive labor. By exposing the disarticulation between time discipline and gestational time, they become "unruly" and hence undesirable workers. In Tanisha and Clarice's longing for a desk job, we can thus read not only their desire for relief from the physicality of service work, but also their hope of upward mobility through classed and racialized labor hierarchies.

Understanding the differential value assigned to the productive and reproductive time of racialized bodies provides one suggestive explanation for the discourses of laziness that emerged in interviews with some frequency. Lovelie St Jean, the Haitian-born home health care worker concerned about her "energy" and the physical demands of her job, responded to my queries about how she was feeling with the exclamation, "I'm lazy!" Her description of a typical day, however, directly contradicted this assertion: she rose around 5:30 each morning, dropped her three-year-old daughter at daycare by seven o'clock, and then took the subway for her twelve-hour shift at her client's home, an hour away, returning late in the evening to do the day's dishes and laundry and fall into bed. On her day or two off a week, she told me, she just wanted to lie around and relax. "I'm just lazy," she repeated.

Of course, the women who employed this term did so at least partially facetiously. Yet, as literary theorists have long reminded us (Bakhtin 2010), words cannot be completely untangled from their histories. In a national culture in which productive work is widely considered the primary condition for full citizenship (Weeks 2011), laziness, understood as the reluctance or lack of desire to work, is not simply a temporary state or one of many traits that make up a person. Rather, it is a moral stain and a strike against claims to citizenship in the political community. The idiom of laziness also resonates with long-standing racist discourses that have accused low-resource Black and brown people of lacking the appropriate work ethic to "pull" themselves out of poverty, and by extension, into "civilized" society. Gender has been central to this discourse; in the rising tide of social conservatism that began under the Reagan administration of the 1980s, women who use any kind of public benefits have been denigrated as "welfare queens" and as freeloaders on public goodwill. In their laziness and dependency, goes the myth, these low-income and always racialized mothers are a primary culprit in perpetuating a "culture of poverty" (Bridges 2011; Greenbaum 2015). By contrast with white and middle-class mothers whose decision to stay at home to raise their children is seen as legitimate and socially important, the reproductive time and labor that low-income women and women of color spend in nurturing and sustaining dependents is dismissed and devalued, especially if they receive government assistance.

Assertions of undesirable reproductive and work ethics—too much time in gestation, too little in productive labor—have thus long been leveled at poor people, particularly those of color (Greenbaum 2015). Perhaps recognizing the racist nature of such discourses, Michaela Johnson, the former retail worker, referenced the concept of laziness in our interview only to immediately reject it. Arguing that her body was only temporarily out of sync with the demands of labor, she explained, "When you're pregnant, you don't wanna work. And it's not your fault fully. You know? Your body pulls back, everything slows down for you. And so it's not that you're lazy. It's the fact that you just cannot do as much as you used to." Pushing back against the discourse of laziness, she points to the body's own will and her lack of volition in controlling the tempo of gestational time. The rhythms of the pregnant body have their own imperatives that cannot be forced into the temporal regimes of service labor.

Scheduling Prenatal Appointments: Navigating the Temporal Regimes of Labor and Clinical Care

The disarticulations between labor time and gestational time were not the only conflicts facing pregnant service workers. Once they decided to begin prenatal care, they also had to navigate the often ponderous bureaucratic time of a safety net public prenatal clinic where appointments were scheduled weeks in advance, sometimes with little input from the patients themselves, and where efforts to contact hospital reception via telephone to reschedule were frustrating and often fruitless.

Pregnant service workers' strategies for attending prenatal appointments, as well as the financial or emotional consequences of attending care, were shaped by the necessity of reconciling the often conflicting forms of temporal governance between their workplaces and clinical care. Since prenatal appointments at Beaumont were almost exclusively offered on weekdays, conflicts were most acute for those with standard work schedules. Although Beaumont did offer Saturday morning appointments twice a month, these were greatly in demand and it was extremely difficult to secure an appointment for these valuable spots. Marlia Singh, a thirty-seven-year-old Guyanese-born home health aide who worked from nine to five every weekday, explained that her agency was contractually obligated to provide care for her client during his scheduled hours. Since partial shifts were not permitted, attending prenatal care meant giving up her entire shift. This resulted in a loss of 20 percent of her weekly income for each prenatal appointment. When I interviewed her in her second trimester, she was already concerned about her ability to navigate labor and clinical time later in her pregnancy when appointments would increase to biweekly in her third trimester and every week in her final month of pregnancy. "I don't get no personal [sick or vacation] days," she explained. "I don't work, I don't get paid. So I don't know how that's going to work. I've got bills to pay, rent to pay. I can't be missing all this work." Although New York City's

Paid Safe and Sick Leave Act guarantees the right to earn paid time off for medical care, it is clear that Marlia is unaware of its provisions. In any case, as we have seen, these hours must be accrued rather than being provided up front, while the law's provision of "up to forty hours" is far less than Marlia would require to compensate her for all of the shifts she would need to miss to attend routine prenatal care.

Attending prenatal care was less fraught for those women with stable and nonstandard schedules, since their schedule reliably included one or more "free" weekdays. Lucia Germaine, the home health aide with a "high-risk" pregnancy, explained, "I work Sunday, Monday, Tuesday, and Wednesday. Then Thursday, Friday, Saturday I'll be off so I'll try to get all my prenatal appointments from Thursday to Friday." Of course, this strategy depended upon the ability or willingness of hospital schedulers to accommodate patients' work rhythms. Although most participants had found Beaumont staff helpful, some also described hospital practices of assigning appointments to women rather than asking their preferences, further complicating attempts to align clinical time with labor time and other commitments. Stéphanie Louis, the twenty-one-year-old home health aide from Haiti, complained, "They just give you the appointment. They don't ask you, 'When is your day off?' They just give it to you and tell you, 'Please come at this time.' And sometimes you feel that it's too hard to change."

Yet, despite the temporal misalignments produced by the occasional indifference of clinical staff, stable schedules mean that conflicts are foreseeable, allowing accommodations to be negotiated with supervisors and co-workers (Clawson and Gerstel 2014; Presser 2003). Health and personal care aides, who made up almost all the participants with stable schedules in my study, usually reported that they would not be penalized for calling out of a shift provided that they gave their supervisor sufficient notice to find a replacement (between twelve and forty-eight hours, depending on the agency). Michelle Walker, a twenty-nine-year-old Jamaican-born home health aide, noted, "They have a lot of aides so one of them will cover for the day while I get my [prenatal] appointment. I just have to do it [inform the supervisor] ahead of time." Given the large reservoir of precarious labor in home health care—aides with insufficient case hours who are willing to accept last-minute shifts to earn extra money—agencies were confident of their ability to find replacements at short notice.

Participants with unstable and unpredictable work schedules reported the most difficulty in reconciling labor time and clinical time. In a typical situation, Jenae Mailler, a twenty-five-year-old US-born cashier at a large supermarket chain, received her schedule on Sunday for the following week. If she discovered a conflict between her shift and her prenatal appointment, she explained,

> I have to sign a grievance to have the days [of work] changed or I have to call and reschedule my [prenatal] appointment. If nobody can fill in for the day that I need to be out, I have to reschedule [the prenatal appointment]. I don't know what my next week's schedule will be, so I have to try to schedule an appointment for some time in that same week. . . . So it's an inconvenience. It's either asking my job for a different day or asking if I can reschedule an appointment.

As we saw in the previous chapter, the temporal precarity produced by unpredictable and last-minute work scheduling is neither natural nor inevitable; it allows employers to maximize profit by making eleventh-hour decisions about staffing ratios (Clawson and Gerstel 2014; Hacker 2006; Lambert 2008). Yet at the same time that pregnant workers were required to flexibly accommodate the demands of labor time, they were also subject to the slow and bureaucratic clinical time of Beaumont Hospital. The lack of synchrony between the temporal rhythms of last-minute labor scheduling and that of public prenatal care produced additional stress, since the clinic usually had little availability for patients hoping to reschedule appointments within the same week. For Jenae, the ability to navigate the temporal regimes of work and prenatal care depended on her warm relationship with her manager and his willingness to accommodate her prenatal appointments to the greatest extent possible when drawing up schedules. In another variation of "working to work" (Standing 2014), Jenae depends on several forms of hidden and unpaid labor—the affective work of cultivating and maintaining relationships with higher-ups as well as the time involved in filling out "grievances" to request schedule changes—to reconcile these conflicting regimes of time.

"Making It Work" (or Not): Relationships with Supervisors and Co-Workers

Expecting the worst, I was pleasantly surprised that almost half of the women I interviewed reported supervisors' and co-workers' willingness to adjust labor time for pregnant employees, often describing them as "caring" (a discourse that we will consider in more detail in chapter 4). In the context of work, care was expressed through supervisors' willingness to adapt work schedules to accommodate prenatal care, as in Jenae's case, or by allowing pregnant employees to take additional bathroom, water, and food breaks. Co-workers also demonstrated care for each other by agreeing to exchange shifts when schedules conflicted with prenatal appointments, by helping with tasks that required heavy or frequent lifting, or simply by asking after their pregnant co-worker's well-being. These workers were the lucky ones, since the slight majority of the participants in this study reported scheduling conflicts between work and medical appointments that sometimes led to acrimonious interactions with supervisors. Michaela Johnson, the discount retail worker, described her manager's resentment at the time commitments entailed in routine prenatal care and the slow pace of clinical time at Beaumont Hospital:

> He'd be like, "Oh what? What is it now? Why are you going [to prenatal care] so frequent?" And I'm like, "I don't know, I've never done this before. The doctor told me I have to come this day, this is the day I have to

come." And he would still try to schedule me. Let's say I said the doctor's appointment is at 1:00, "Well, how long you think you're gonna be there?" I'm like, "I don't know how long this appointment is gonna take." He'd put me in a jam, [saying] "Oh, well, be here by 3:00." Well, I didn't get out of my appointment until 3:00 or 3:30 and now I'm late for my shift. . . . That was extra stress, and I was like, "I don't want to do that to my child."

In his refusal to acknowledge her powerlessness to either predict or expedite the pace of clinical time, Michaela's supervisor exacerbated the discordance between the temporal regimes of work and public prenatal care, as well as the stress and frustration produced by these disjunctures. Fearing that these negative affective states might directly affect her developing fetus, Michaela pointed to her maternal obligation to care for her future child as a powerful factor in her decision to leave her position.

Pregnant service workers are thus vulnerable to punitive labor practices if they are unable to reconcile the "arrhythmia" (Lefebvre 2004) between labor time, clinical time, and gestational time. Two of the fifty-five women in my study, both employed as line chefs, had been fired after informing their managers of their pregnancy, a practice that they knew was illegal but lacked the will or the resources to fight. More commonly, supervisors reluctant to schedule around prenatal appointments or to accommodate the needs of pregnant workers accomplished the same effect through reductions in hours so dramatic that women eventually quit "of their own choice," recognizing the unsustainable investment of time and money required to attend a shift that might not even cover their expenses. In yet another example of bad faith, several women also told me that their employers had informed them that this forced curtailing of labor time would benefit them by allowing them to "put their pregnancy first." Faced with unsympathetic work environments, participants often indicated their willingness to leave their positions rather than seek remediation through official channels, contributing to the often noted high turnover rate among service sector workers (Boushey 2016). While resolving immediate conflicts, such responses have other negative consequences, resulting in a loss of income as well as "turning back the clock" on any benefits, such as promotions or paid sick leave, that women may have accrued through time on the job.

In workplaces where managers were unable or unwilling to arrange labor time around women's prenatal appointments, co-workers often represented a key source of support. Research on the understudied role of co-workers in workplace flexibility has found that co-workers are often motivated to accommodate each other, particularly colleagues with whom they have a good relationship (Clawson and Gerstel 2014; Henly, Shaefer, and Waxman 2006). Financial motivations may play a part; given low wages and the all-too-frequent "scramble for hours" (Ray 2018), co-workers are often happy to take on additional shifts. Maureen Robinson, a home health aide originally from Jamaica, worked a twelve-hour shift from Thursdays to Sundays with a client who required twenty-four-hour care. If she was unable to schedule prenatal care on her days off, she had a standing arrangement to offer her shift first to the aide who worked the night shift before alerting the supervisor. She told me, "I could talk to the other lady and she would come in for me. We cover for each other. We switch. Everybody wants money, so she prefers to get the pay than somebody else."

But motivations were not only financial, as people may "swap" or exchange shifts in ways that have no direct economic benefit. Tasha Washington, the cashier at a fast-food restaurant, described the difficulties of attending prenatal care given her wildly unpredictable work schedule.

> TASHA: Sometimes it's kind of hard. But when you have co-workers that understand, they help you out. But it's a struggle. You don't want to put stuff on other people that has nothing to do with them. Even though you're working with them, you still have to work around. You take mine and I have to take yours. But it might not be better for me, so now I have to find somebody else to take that [shift]. It's a struggle.
> ELISE: So you can make it work because you have good co-workers, not because your employer is helpful.

TASHA: Yeah, my manager [says] "Oh, there's nothing I can do." All they can do is tell you to advertise it. If you can't advertise it [and have someone pick up the shift], then I don't know. There is no type of help.

Swapping shifts can thus be driven by altruism—the desire to help a co-worker—as well as by often unspoken expectations of reciprocity. As Marcel Mauss ([1925] 1954) pointed out a century ago, a gift received must always be returned; for shift workers, agreeing to work a shift for a colleague begins a cycle of debt and the obligation to return the favor. As Tasha puts it, "You take mine and I have to take yours." But Tasha also notes that there are also limits to what can be asked of co-workers, since taking an unexpected and last-minute shift requires disruptions to their own plans and commitments. Moreover, swapping shifts may not always resolve temporal conflicts; Tasha may swap with a co-worker to attend prenatal care only to realize that she is unable to work the co-worker's shift. The process would then begin anew, forcing her to petition others to cover the shift or to advertise it and hope that someone would pick it up. Should these fail, she must renege on her previous commitment and work the agreed-upon shift or call out and be penalized through loss of income and company demerits. As Dan Clawson and Naomi Gerstel (2014) observe, reliance on the goodwill of co-workers to navigate the temporal governance of service workplaces often increases workers' resentment of workplace hierarchies. The claims of frontline managers that "they can do nothing" to ease lower-level workers' temporal conflicts, whether true or not, is a reminder that it is co-workers rather than higher-ups or workplace policy that make it possible to navigate rigid and inflexible labor regimes.

Service workers' labor vulnerability during pregnancy thus underscores the stakes of what medical anthropologists have called "the politics of disclosure," or decisions about whether and whom to tell about potentially stigmatizing conditions (Goffman [1963] 1986; Inhorn 1986). For pregnant service workers, the politics of disclosure entailed deciding when, or sometimes even whether, to tell supervisors and co-workers about their pregnancies. Some women delayed as long as possible, fearing employers' reactions, while a few home health aides, particularly those with little in-person contact with supervisors and good relationships with long-term clients, told me that they did not plan to inform their agencies at all. Their concerns were not unusual: a national study of pregnant people found that 21 percent feared informing their employer about their pregnancy because of possible discrimination or retaliation (Gitis, Sprick, and Schweer 2022). For the women I interviewed, weighing the politics of disclosure was contingent upon their assessment of their ability to successfully reconcile the discordance between labor time and gestational time, and their evaluation of the extent to which clients, supervisors, and co-workers "cared" for them and their pregnancies.

Forced Choices: Work or Prenatal Care?

Despite their efforts to arrange schedules to accommodate both their work obligations and medical appointments, pregnant service sector workers may be faced with situations in which they are forced to choose between keeping a shift and attending prenatal care. These temporal conflicts were unintentionally exacerbated by changes in temporal governance at Beaumont Hospital. When I began research, some providers were still willing to see walk-in patients on a first-come, first-served basis. But as administrators grappled with the problem of chronic backlogs and delays that plagued the obstetrics department (which we will see in the next chapter), this option was eliminated. According to Dr. Silva, administrators and clinic staff felt that walk-in patients were a major contributor to the problem; patients without appointments would be waiting outside even before the clinic opened, overloading providers and delaying care for patients who had scheduled appointments later in the day. Although intended to improve patient experience by streamlining "flow" and minimizing delays, the termination of the walk-in option presented a further obstacle to prenatal care, especially for women with unstable and unpredictable work schedules.

In this context, some participants—particularly first-time mothers and those with other sources of financial support—were adamant that prenatal care should take priority over work, even at the expense of income or the goodwill of clients or supervisors. Nyanna Jones, the retail assistant manager of the previous chapter who had inquired about her eligibility for the FMLA, described her manager's reluctance to accommodate her prenatal care during the busy period of training new hires. "I called out today," she declared, "because my appointment is important. My job is important also but my baby comes first. . . . I told the hospital that I'm only available for appointments on Tuesdays and Thursdays, but it doesn't always work out. So that will be five hours [paid time] today that I would have gotten but for the scheduling." Similarly, Abigail Fletcher, a thirty-seven-year-old home health aide with two adolescents in her home country of Grenada, told me, "I'm hoping they [her clients/supervisor] do not react funny, because even if they do, I'm gonna decide, well, it's gonna be my baby. I will do what I have to do. Because this baby, I been looking for—I been through a couple losses [miscarriages], three of them, before I get this child."

As these commentaries reveal, those women who stated that they would prioritize prenatal appointments did not do so by asserting their legal right to time to seek medical care. Rather, they defended their decision by referencing their role as (future) mothers and their obligation to care for the health and well-being of their children. When Nyanna Jones's manager requested that she delay her already scheduled appointment in order to help to train new employees, for example, she recalled her response: "Listen, it's not about me or you, it's about my baby and I know I have to be at the doctor's today. That's where I'm going to go. I cannot make it today." In asserting the moral claims of future children over the demands of labor time, women like Nyanna and Michaela drew on culturally shared ideologies about their responsibility as mothers to make claims for accommodations that might not have been countenanced if it had "just" been about their own health. Moral claims to care were thus made in several temporal registers as women argued for accommodations not (only) on their own behalf but in the name of their fetuses.

Other participants made different decisions, stating that they would choose to delay prenatal care rather than giving up a shift. Since missing a work shift means a loss of income, these tended to be women with greater financial responsibilities or more fragile economic support systems, especially those with other children and single mothers with limited familial help. Shanelle Tompkins, a US-born home health aide and single mother of two, said simply, "I have to go to work. I started my prenatal care late [at four and a half months] because, you know, you have to work. You have bills to pay."

Most of the women with whom I spoke, however, narrated complex and shifting assessments of priorities as they engaged in an ongoing negotiation between the temporal regimes of labor and prenatal care and the progression of gestational time. Lucia Germaine, the home health aide with a medically "high-risk" pregnancy, initially declared, "I feel that my prenatal is more important than anything right now. My job is important but it's a prenatal appointment. I don't want to miss any of those." Yet, almost immediately, she qualified her assertion, stating, "Well, I have to be focused on both [job and prenatal care]. I need the money because I'm about to have a baby. I don't want to lose my job because I called out too much, so I try to work with them [clients and supervisors]." While attending biomedical prenatal appointments is one way that pregnant people can enact cultural expectations about maternal care for the fetus (e.g., Andaya 2014; Gálvez 2011; Waggoner 2017), Lucia was also sharply aware of the necessity of working in order to save for the unpaid weeks or months after she gave birth. This economic rationale, in which a "good mother" provides for her children, is another form of culturally valued maternal care. In her narrative oscillation, Lucia thus articulates the tension as the discrepant and inflexible temporal regimes of labor and prenatal care force her to make untenable choices between caring for her physical health and caring for her economic well-being.

Cultural ideologies of motherhood and the gendered responsibility for children thus profoundly shape the reach of employers' power over workers' time, although not in any predetermined direction. Among the women I interviewed, the presence of dependent children in the household was the most-cited reason for decisions to both accept undesirable schedules and to refuse them. For single mothers or those with extremely limited economic supports, as was the case with Tanisha, the need to provide for children was the primary reason for accepting unwanted schedules and prioritizing work over prenatal care (Carrillo et al. 2017; Presser 2003). For others, ideologies of maternal care also provide a socially and personally legitimated reason to refuse to take shifts that might negatively affect the well-being of their (future) children (Clawson and Gerstel 2014; Coe 2019).

Conclusion

Writing of call center workers in India, Purnima Mankekar and Akhil Gupta observe that "time discipline [does] not act uniformly on bodies" (2019, 420); its effects are deeply shaped by factors such as gender, class, race/ethnicity, parental status, and so forth. As the accounts in this chapter highlight, pregnancy and the arc of gestational time at times produced acute conflicts for workers as they attempted to navigate both the classed and racialized time discipline of service work and the temporal governance of prenatal care. In this context, the willingness of supervisors and co-workers to make accommodations for pregnant workers was interpreted as evidence of their care, or lack thereof. Supervisors who cared were those who acknowledged the needs of women's changing bodies over the duration of their pregnancies and its incompatibility with rigid forms of time discipline. Conversely, those who "didn't care" were those who expected women to labor on as if nothing had changed—that is, to continue attuning their bodies to the physical and temporal regimes of service work as if they were not also shaped by the arc of gestational time.

Attitudes and relationships also shifted over time. As pregnancies developed, situations that supervisors and managers might have been willing to accommodate during the early weeks of pregnancy could become conflictive as women's larger and slower bodies and the demands of *in vivo* time threatened the rigid and regulated temporal regimes of low-wage service work, while the ever-increasing number of prenatal visits increased pregnant workers' subjection to the vagaries of clinical time. As we will consider in the next chapter, women's efforts to navigate labor and gestational time were often complicated by the bureaucratic and unpredictable workings of clinical time at Beaumont Hospital.

3

Clinical Time and Racialized Inequality in Safety Net Prenatal Care

It was a stifling August day and the cooling system in the prenatal care suite at Beaumont Hospital was struggling, largely unsuccessfully, to combat the oppressive heat and humidity outside. As usual, the waiting room was overflowing with pregnant women waiting for their appointments. Today was a particularly bad day: a midwife and a nurse-practitioner in the clinical suite dedicated to low-risk pregnancies had called out sick and other providers, including two doctors who normally exclusively handled high-risk cases such as pregnant women with gestational diabetes, high blood pressure, or previous caesarian sections, had been asked to absorb the patient load. Receptionists were instructed to accept only obstetric visits and to reschedule any patient with non-urgent gynecological concerns, sometimes delivering this unwelcome news to women already registered and waiting for their appointment. Both patients and clinic staff were feeling the strain; as Dr. Silva hurried past on a quick bathroom break, she muttered in an aside to me, "Not only is it stinking hot back there [in the providers' rooms], but everyone is overworked, overtired, and underfed."

In this tense atmosphere, patients waited, listlessly fanning themselves with the literature distributed during the morning's breastfeeding class. Finally, a pregnant patient in blue scrubs, clearly on her own way to or from a work shift, approached the hospital educator whom I was shadowing and told her that she had been waiting for an hour for her PPD (purified protein derivative, a skin test for latent tuberculosis). The midwife in charge of her care overheard her, and apologetically admitted that she had forgotten to put this order into the nurses' system in the chaos. A nurse was called but could not attend the woman because she was already busy tending to a pregnant patient suffering from heat exhaustion. The woman sighed deeply and exclaimed, "I'm dying out there [in the waiting room]. I'm dying. You don't understand." Immediately, both nurse and midwife chided her, "Don't say that. You don't say you're dying. That's a terrible thing to say here." Only slightly repentant, the woman modified her statement: "I'm suffering out there. I can't be here anymore." Acknowledging my sympathetic gaze, she sighed, "It's like a broken record here. Every time, the same thing. I can't take it anymore."

In some ways, this is a familiar picture of conditions in the safety net health institutions that predominantly serve urban communities of color: stressed and overworked providers, uncomfortable conditions, and disgruntled patients (e.g., Goldstein 2022). Such depictions are not unfounded. During my fieldwork, I observed inefficiencies and practices that lengthened patient wait times as well as, less commonly, encounters where clinic staff were openly dismissive of patient complaints about delays. Yet I also daily witnessed the effort of staff from receptionists to medical professionals who worked to provide quality care and attention in a public safety net hospital that was oversubscribed, underfunded, and too often constrained by political and economic decision making outside the control of administrators and medical staff.

An important body of literature has examined racism in medical practice, showing how racial stereotypes and assumptions directly and negatively impact quality of care (Bridges 2011; D. Davis 2019; Hoberman 2012). Ethnographies of healthcare in safety net facilities have also made note of "racial geograph[ies]" (Bridges 2011, 11) in which a largely white medical staff attends to a low-income patient population predominantly comprised of Black and brown people. By contrast, most of the staff at Beaumont's prenatal clinic would be socially identified as Black, from receptionists and PCAs (patient care associates) to nurses, midwives, and some doctors. It is outside the scope of this study to determine the degree to which hospital culture was shaped by this largely shared racial background, since class and educational status can be just as salient categories of difference and hierarchy as that of the social construction of "race." While some providers were certainly more committed to giving courteous and quality care than others, my focus is not on revealing instances of individual racism in care delivery. Rather, we will consider how the forms of temporal governance that shape clinical time, as well as the unequal distribution of resources that often drive these policies and practices, directly reflect and reproduce broader racial hierarchies and racialized systems of value.

This chapter examines how clinical time, or the bureaucratic temporal regimes and forms of temporal governance in clinical settings, shaped pregnant service workers' experience of safety net prenatal care. In the seeming inescapability of waiting and the necessity of enduring long and often inexplicable delays, pregnant women often felt an institutional lack of care for their well-being even as they received the technical care of prenatal monitoring and management. But these same temporal structures constrained conditions of practice for providers as well, who felt pressured to provide care under constant time pressure and few resources. Inequality is thus instantiated and experienced through racialized and classed temporal structures, producing patients and providers who both experience their lesser value in broader social hierarchies.

Reproducing Racial Inequality: The Dismantling of New York City's Public Healthcare System

Conditions of safety net healthcare in New York City, as well as the entrenched and growing reproductive health disparities that we saw in the book's introduction, are a direct result of decades of racialized policies of economic austerity that have undermined systems of care for low-income communities. In the early part of the twentieth century, the city's robust network of public and independent hospitals and clinics served a wide swathe of the population, not only those considered poor or indigent (Opdycke 1999; Oshinsky 2016). The fiscal crisis of the 1970s, however, sharply exacerbated racial and economic divides; middle-class white families departed for the city's whiter and more affluent suburbs while poor residents of color, trapped by racist practices of redlining and housing discrimination, were left in deteriorating inner-city neighborhoods.[1] As New York City became increasingly comprised of residents of color, dominant attitudes among (white) policy makers and legislators shifted from viewing social services as a right to seeing them as largesse subsidized by white taxpayers that were being used and possibly abused by families of color (Phillips-Fein 2017; see also Briggs 2017). The more that public healthcare was associated with Black and brown communities, the louder came the calls for funding cuts. In an example of "dog whistle politics" whereby "coded rhetoric, that does not seem to be overtly about race, mobilizes white racial fears to reject social programs that are perceived as benefitting minorities" (Mulligan 2017, 133), the racialization of public healthcare and its defunding were inextricably intertwined.

This history starkly illustrates the workings of what Michelle Murphy calls the "economization of life," by which she means "a historically specific regime of valuation created with technoscientific practices ... that calibrate[s] and then exploit[s] the differential worth of human life for the sake of the macrological figure of the 'economy'" (2017, 6). Through ostensibly unavoidable cost-cutting measures, policy makers have safeguarded the city's economic well-being by allocating fewer material and human resources to institutions that predominantly serve Black and brown people. Over decades of financial and moral divestment, the healthcare system has been divided into, on the one hand, private institutions where white(ned) and wealthier bodies are nurtured and cared for and, on the other, a system of safety net care for poorer and racialized bodies.

In low-resource neighborhoods, where private doctors' offices are a rarity, safety net hospitals play a crucial role; in 2017, one neighborhood in Brooklyn had only two non-hospital-based primary care physicians per ten thousand residents, compared with more than sixty per ten thousand residents in a similar geographic area on Manhattan's East Side

(Goldstein 2022). Yet since 2003, more than fifteen hospitals that primarily served low-income, minority, and immigrant neighborhoods—the very communities that would later be devastated by the COVID-19 pandemic—have closed in New York City, putting more pressure on remaining facilities and increasing both travel and wait times for the patients they serve. Those safety net hospitals that remain continue to be chronically strained by inadequate state and federal budgets, low reimbursements from Medicaid and other insurers, and a high proportion of uninsured patients (many of whom are undocumented immigrants who are ineligible for either public or private insurance coverage).[2] In 2016 a report by then mayor Bill de Blasio's administration noted that the funding gap produced by shrinking state and federal funds, as well as a large uninsured and underinsured patient population, had forced the city's safety net healthcare system to "the edge of a financial cliff" (Ransom 2018).

The economization of public health thus functions by exploiting the unequal value of racialized life, producing apparently natural environments of scarcity that force constant triaging of care. In this context of "racist neoliberalism" (Briggs 2017), low-income communities of color are exhorted to "take responsibility" for their health, and their poorer health outcomes are blamed on their own "bad choices," even as local and federal governments slash the budgets of institutions that are supposed to care for them. This long-term disinvestment into safety net healthcare institutions means that low-income pregnant women encounter a stressed system with providers who must give care under chronically resource-strapped conditions. These temporal regimes cause stress and distress to both patients and providers; patients endure long waits that they see as evidence of a lack of respect for their time while providers feel rushed, overburdened, under-resourced, and unappreciated for *their* time. As we will see, these disparate experiences of time are entangled and mutually constituted in racialized structures of inequality that constrain conditions of care.

Waiting: Patients' Experiences of Temporal Governance in the Clinic

At Beaumont Hospital, as in other public prenatal clinics that I visited around the city, waiting was an unavoidable aspect of seeking care; pregnant patients could easily wait for ninety minutes or more for a provider visit that lasted fewer than fifteen minutes. Yet women generally endured wait times patiently, passing the time with games or social media apps on their phones, dozing fitfully in the hard plastic chairs, listening absent-mindedly to health educators' presentations on breastfeeding and safe infant sleeping practices, or staring at videos on diabetes and surgical wound care that played on a continuous loop on the waiting room's small television. Only when wait times extended an hour or more past scheduled appointments did patients start to stir and complain quietly under their breath.

The waiting room was relatively quiet on this particular morning, although the line of women waiting to check in for their appointments was beginning to build as the sole receptionist on duty, Ms. Hayworth, worked steadily to open electronic check-in records, process paperwork, answer the telephone, and direct patients to the correct suite. A pregnant woman approached the desk; she just needed to have her bloodwork done today and could be sent straight to the laboratory, but she wanted to ask her provider a question. Ms. Hayworth told her to take a seat and went back to the examination rooms to alert the provider, who was occupied with another patient. Forty minutes passed. Finally, the woman approached the reception desk again to request the return of her clinic identification card that is required for all medical appointments at the hospital. "On Monday, I was here at 9:30 a.m. and didn't leave until 7:00 p.m.," she declared. "They ain't gonna do that to me again." I offered to go to the provider's office to retrieve the clinic card, but when I knocked on the door, the provider indicated that she could now speak to the patient. Despite my concern that both might be feeling aggrieved (the patient by her wait and the provider by needing to fit in an unscheduled patient), I heard them greet each other warmly as the door closed behind them.

The patient left the provider's office about ten minutes later and stopped by the front desk for a WIC form, since medical confirmation of pregnancy and expected date of delivery are required for this federally subsidized food program. These forms must be filled out by a nurse, and Ms. Hayworth hesitated before replying, "It's going to take a while, and I know you can't wait . . ." Impatiently, the woman responded, "It's not that I *can't* wait today. It's that everywhere you go here you've got to wait. You go to [financial] clearance, you've got to wait; you go to the nutritionist, you wait; you see a nurse, you wait; you want a WIC form, you wait." With a frustrated shake of her head, she reiterated, "I was here 9:30 a.m. to 7:00 p.m. on Monday and I can't do that again." Ms. Hayworth looked at her, not unsympathetically, and replied, "I understand. You're justified in feeling that way."

Beaumont Hospital is not unique. Research on state bureaucracies around the world has repeatedly found that waiting has become virtually synonymous with services for the poor, reflecting wider hierarchies of value in which poor people's time is assumed to be less valuable than that of wealthier individuals as well as the implicit belief that they *should* wait for the services that they are receiving "for free" (Andaya 2017; Auyero 2012; Chary et al. 2016; Gupta 2012; Lowry 2021). In the hierarchical organization of clinical time, by contrast, doctors' time is a valuable commodity to be optimized for maximum efficiency and profit (Clawson and Gerstel 2014; McCourt 2013; Zerubavel 1979). Feminist scholars working in the field of reproduction have argued that the temporal organization of biomedical obstetric care prioritizes doctors' time over that of laboring women, resulting in high rates of caesarian sections and reiterating gendered hierarchies in which (male) medical time, status, and knowledge are valued over pregnant people's autonomy and embodied experience (Davis-Floyd 2004; Martin 1987; McCourt 2013). Anthropologists working in a number of sites have also examined how bureaucratic policies and practices, including temporal control, regulate access to reproductive care for women marked as Other by virtue of race/ethnicity, class, incarceration record, and so forth (Knight 2015; Martínez 2018; Singer 2022; Smith-Oka 2009; Strong 2020; Sufrin 2017).

At Beaumont, as with other hospital settings, the relationship between status and waiting is quite clear. Not everybody waits. Doctors hurry from room to room, their quick steps easily distinguishable from the slower gait of patients and other hospital staff, and clinical procedures and the structure of patient flow are designed to minimize any waiting that might "waste" their valuable time (Clawson and Gerstel 2014; Saunders 2010). Nurses play a key role in patient care, but they wait too for doctors and other providers. The PCAs (patient care associates), who take patients' vital signs and prepare them for their provider encounter, wait for doctors to finish with existing patients and vacate rooms, a process over which they have no control. And patients—at Beaumont, almost exclusively low-income people of color—wait for everybody, their largely immobile and apparently quiescent bodies a stark contrast to the constant ebb and flow of the hospital staff around them.

Although the experience of waiting for the doctor, and the accompanying recognition that doctors' time is considered more valuable than that of their patients, is widely shared across class divides, safety net hospitals in New York City are notorious for their long wait times. In 2016 an internal time study conducted by Beaumont's obstetrics department found that appointment cycle times (from registration to the end of the appointment) exceeded target times by 111 percent, and both internal reports and my own interviews found that the length of time spent waiting was the most-voiced complaint about the hospital's prenatal services. On one morning, Cleo Mason, a twenty-one-year-old woman from Jamaica pregnant with her first child, settled with a sigh into one of the wooden school chairs in the interview room after leaving her provider's office. Without preamble, she declared, "Today was the first day that I wasn't exasperated and crying after my appointment." She usually made her appointment for a Friday, which was her day off from her job as an aide on the dementia floor of a nursing home. Unbeknownst to her, Mondays and Fridays were notorious for delays and overcrowding. According to providers, these weekly rhythms were produced by the fact that anyone who wanted or needed to call out of a shift, whether patients or providers, preferred to do so on the days abutting the weekends, resulting in large numbers of patients waiting for fewer providers. "Last time," Cleo went on, "I had an appointment at 11:40. I was here on time and I didn't leave till 5:40! I was so mad. They told me, 'Oh, there was a mistake with your provider.' I just told them, 'What kind of mistake? What do you mean, 'there's been a mistake,' when I've been sitting here for hours for an appointment that doesn't even last ten minutes?'" Upset by this encounter, on the day that we spoke she had called out of a Tuesday shift and had finished her appointment in two and a half hours, a rather quick time for Beaumont.

To some extent, Beaumont's lengthy prenatal visits reflect Medicaid's numerous prenatal screening requirements for low-income pregnant women, who are required to undergo screening on topics from intimate partner violence to sexual partnerships, housing, nutrition, and household budgets in initial and some subsequent visits. A benevolent reading suggests that such screenings are necessary to ensure that pregnant women have access to needed information and services, at least for the duration of their pregnancies. Yet these personal and sometimes intrusive questions are never demanded of privately insured pregnant women. This discrepancy calls attention to the racializing logic informing publicly insured prenatal care: the maternal capabilities of low-income women, coded as nonwhite, are seen as simultaneously suspect and under threat, with their pregnancies perceived to be endangered by their own poor choices and behaviors as well as by their relationships and social conditions (Andaya 2017; Bridges 2011; D. Davis 2019; Gálvez 2011).

However well-intentioned, the social and medical policies that inform temporal governance at Beaumont are inextricably intertwined with broader ideologies and systems of inequality: low-income women are perceived as in need of time-intensive medical and social surveillance but also shunted to under-resourced institutions where they are forced to wait long hours for care. These delays and backlogs in turn convey contradictory discourses about the importance of patients' time and the value of their pregnancies. Given constructions of knowledge that portray low-income women and women of color as both medically "high risk" and socially "at risk," public health and medical messaging encourages them to become good risk-reducing maternal subjects by accessing "timely" and regular prenatal care (Rose 2007). Yet when they do seek care through the safety net health system, they are often met with long delays that suggest that their time and effort in attending prenatal appointments do not matter.

The racialized and classed nature of clinical temporal governance was reiterated in other ways too. One midwife, Joanna, who had recently left her position at a different safety net hospital, described the institutional practice of assigning women prenatal appointments without regard for their preexisting schedules:

> They make her an appointment which usually has absolutely nothing to do with that patient's actual availability. They say, "Okay, you need to be seen in two weeks. Two weeks from today is such-and-such date. This is the time we have available. Here's your appointment." Was there any point at which you wanted to check in with that woman to see if she's available to come at that time? No, not usually. Because they're poor. Because most of them are not white. Because most of them don't speak English. Because most of them are not citizens. Because none of them are paying. I think the attitude is, "You're getting free care so you're going to take what we give you and you're going to be grateful. And if you're not, we're going to roll our eyes at you because, 'What do you expect?'" ... Their time isn't valued.

Her passionate commentary highlights how inequality is reproduced through bureaucratic practices of temporal governance, such as the scheduling of appointments, that depend upon performances of neutrality but in fact often reflect raced and classed assumptions about pregnant patients and their time. Occupying multiple positions of marginality—poor, nonwhite, often immigrant, sometimes non-English-speaking—women are expected not only to accommodate their own schedules to the temporal demands of the hospital but also to be grateful for the "charity" care they receive, whenever that happens to take place.

At Beaumont, by contrast with Joanna's former hospital, I generally observed reception staff trying to accommodate women's scheduling preferences (although, as we saw in the previous chapter, this was not always the case). However, the volume of patients that the hospital served with limited resources often made this impossible, and women were sometimes assigned to appointments that they already knew would be extremely difficult to attend. Not infrequently, I observed women glancing with consternation at the clinic card that was returned to them at the conclusion of every appointment with the time of their next appointment written on the back. When they returned to the receptionist to tell her that their work or childcare obligations would mean that they could likely not arrive for the appointment on time, they were often told to "try your hardest" since there were no other appointments available that week to fit their schedule. The time and effort that women expended to attend prenatal appointments were visible only when women "failed" to show up or arrived late to appointments, and when their perceived "choice" not to attend prenatal care risked reproducing stereotypes about the at-risk and noncompliant maternal subject.

In making explicit the widespread assumption that the time of poor people should be reorganized to accommodate the schedules of status superiors, temporal governance in the clinic reiterates long-standing social ideologies that hold that the time of certain racialized, classed, and gendered subjects is not as valuable as that of others. Through the disciplinary power of clinical temporal governance and the apparent lack of concern for their own productive and reproductive time, pregnant women thus experience their unequal position as racialized and classed "patients of the state" (Auyero 2012; see also Martínez 2018; Singer 2022).

Time Seizures and the Failures of Care

The unpredictable temporal workings of the clinic, where appointment times often bore little relation to when women were actually seen, also accentuated the disjunctures between clinical time and the other temporal regimes that governed patients' lives. On one occasion, a woman who had been waiting for over two and a half hours to see her provider stalked up to Ms. Hayworth, the receptionist, to complain loudly about the delay. Ms. Hayworth was courteous and responsive, but ultimately powerless to speed up the pace of care. Defeated, the woman returned to her seat, declaring, "I have to go to work. They don't respect my time!" At this, a murmur of sympathy went up from the watching patients, slowly quietening as they each went back to the ongoing (in)activity of waiting.

In their complaints about wait times, some participants in this research explicitly pointed to the economic costs of long delays, viewing delays as a lack of institutional and provider respect for the value of their time. Working in the Harlem neighborhood of New York City, Philippe Bourgois (2003) has argued that the discourse of respect is a culturally resonant framework through which low-resource members of urban communities of color demand recognition as equals in a deeply stratified social and economic order. In the prenatal clinic, the idiom of respect appeared frequently as a language through which patients protested the unfairness of systems that devalued their time. Jasmine Tremain, the fashion retail employee, told me that she was committed to attending prenatal care no matter what: "My child comes first," she declared. "Having a healthy baby is the most important thing." Yet, still only in her second appointment at Beaumont, she had already found the wait times at Beaumont exasperating and swore to me that it was the last time that she would go there for care. At her previous appointment, she had waited for four hours for the lab to confirm her pregnancy even though it had already been confirmed by her primary care physician (in-house confirmation of pregnancy is required for Medicaid reimbursement, highlighting the additional time demands and surveillance experienced by publicly insured pregnant people). Adding to her indignation, today's appointment had already taken over three hours and she had found her provider dismissive to the point of rudeness. Underscoring the delays that forced her to squander time that she could otherwise be using for her economic benefit, she exclaimed,

> In this time, I could've grabbed a shift, I could have made some money with this time, but I wanted to put my baby first. It's my first, so you know, I'm nervous, I want to make sure my baby is OK. But I still haven't received any prenatal care. I haven't advanced myself in the process. I had a 1:00 p.m. appointment. It's now 4:00 p.m. and I'm still here [waiting for the PCA to schedule her next appointment]. . . . Today I lost a day's work to come and I still don't know anything. The provider wouldn't even tell me my due date. She told me that the person who took my vitals would give me all that information, plus my next appointment. But I'm not coming back. They don't respect my time.

For Jasmine, each hour expended in the black box of clinical time is a potential hour of paid labor time. Studies suggest that given their earning structure, hourly-waged workers are more likely than salaried workers to directly monetize their time, and to weigh economic considerations strongly when considering trade-offs between time and money (DeVoe and Pfeffer 2007). Further, as Amy Cooper (2015) argues in her research on service-seeking among unhoused women, the feeling of powerlessness produced by the inability to reconcile the conflicting schedules of service providers undercuts the very foundation of personhood in American society—the possession of an agentive and autonomous self. Jasmine, for example, was prepared for some loss of economically productive time to attend prenatal appointments, demonstrating "proper" maternal care by putting "her baby first." Faced with ever-extending wait times and her provider's refusal to share basic information, however, she began to perceive the clinical encounter as disrespectful of the value of both her time and her person. In this context, her decision to seek prenatal care elsewhere is a means of (re)asserting her agency and her right to respectful and timely clinical interactions.

While some women denounced the unfairness of clinical temporal regimes that wasted their time for income-earning activity, others bemoaned its interference with other time-sensitive commitments, such as responsibilities to children and to household work. On the day that I interviewed her, Clarice Taylor, the pregnant accountant turned nanny, had been waiting for more than three hours to be seen for her ten o'clock appointment. She declared, "I'm just here waiting. You get nothing done, no laundry, no shopping. And you know," she went on regretfully, "my baby [her seven-year-old daughter] knows I took off today, so she's like, 'Can you pick me up at 2:20 [when school lets out], mommy?' Because you know I never can. And I'm looking at the time now, I'm just like, 'Nope. No, I can't. I'm sorry, baby.' Sitting here, you just waste your day." Hours spent waiting in crowded safety net prenatal clinics thus not only produced conflicts with labor time, but also with the temporal rhythms of home and kin groups. For many, these "time seizures" (A. Cooper 2015) engendered feelings of frustration and powerlessness, reinforcing perceptions of an institutional lack of care and respect for patients' time.

But the economic discourse of "wasted" time was not the only language that participants employed to protest their place at the lower ranks of Beaumont's temporal hierarchy. In other cases, women expressed a moral indignation at the bodily suffering produced by clinical temporal regimes. Dana Persaud, a forty-one-year-old home health aide from Guyana, shook her head as she remembered the travails of her previous appointment at Beaumont: "The other day I was here, I came here [at] ten o'clock, and I did not leave here until three o'clock. All day you are here. Sometimes you're hungry and you just need to go get something to eat, and you cannot even move because somebody will call you [for the appointment] and you're not there." Shanelle Tompkins, a pregnant twenty-three-year-old mother of two employed as a home health aide for her disabled father, echoed this sentiment, declaring in annoyance,

"We are pregnant, you can't have us stressing out. I've been here hours. I'm starving, but I don't want to run downstairs [to the cafeteria] in case they call me. It's not right. I'm pregnant and it's like they don't care about me or my baby."

Through such embodied complaints, patients denounced the injustice of temporal regimes that made them wait. As the women I interviewed were at pains to underscore, these were not generic or universal bodies; these were *pregnant* people who were forced into immobility, struggling to stay comfortable in the upright plastic chairs and enduring hunger rather than risk missing their appointments. They thus asserted the moral imperative of considering pregnancy as a time-limited state during which otherwise indifferent bureaucratic structures should care for pregnant women by shielding them from the ill-effects of hunger, stress, and fatigue. In the absence of such consideration, articulations of discomfort in the waiting room could be occasions for expressions of solidarity and the circulation of knowledge among waiting patients. At times, I heard women offer to let clinic staff know that a woman had left only temporarily or provide advice to a new patient on the most likely time to catch the nutritional counselor or social worker. Yet such overtures, while appreciated, had little power to influence the temporal regimes that shaped experiences of waiting in the clinic, a fact of which women were acutely aware.

The sometimes painfully slow and indifferent workings of clinical time thus produced negative physical and affective states—hunger, boredom, stress, frustration, and anger—that underscored women's vulnerability to temporal regimes and forms of temporal governance over which they had little control. In pointing to their suffering, women drew attention to the fact that the provision of technical care—weighing, measuring, and monitoring maternal and fetal bodies—did not always make them feel *cared for* (Caldwell 2017; Sufrin 2017). Through practices of social distancing that range from detachment to outright hostility, patients can perceive a lack of caring through the very provision of medical care intended to sustain the biological health of pregnant person and fetus.

Clinical encounters can thus instantiate and reproduce social inequality as often as they produce relationships of care (Foucault 1982). Of course, such experiences were not universal; about one-third of my participants said that they were willing to tolerate the wait times, either because they liked their provider and felt that they were receiving good care or because they simply considered it an inevitable aspect of accessing safety net services for the poor. In other cases, however, women voted with their feet. One afternoon when the line to check in at the registration desk was moving exceptionally slowly, a woman who had been tapping her foot impatiently suddenly stepped out of the queue, declaring loudly, "I'm going to get [prenatal] care somewhere else. I don't feel the love here." Taken aback, the usually cordial receptionist, Ms. Hernández, murmured to me, "She doesn't feel the love? Well, there's plenty of others who do."

Racing Time: The Provider Perspective

Whether produced by overburdened facilities or through practices of indifference, clinical temporal regimes bear the imprint of broader processes that reaffirm the inferior position of low-income people and communities of color in social and political hierarchies. Yet it was not only patients who objected to the long wait times; clinical staff and administrators often expressed frustration at the persistence of delays despite their attempts to ameliorate this problem. In the context of always constrained state and federal support for public and safety net healthcare, prenatal patients at Beaumont were in great demand because of the Medicaid dollars that they brought to the hospital (since uninsured pregnant people are eligible for Medicaid-funded prenatal and postpartum care in New York State). The obstetrics department was the only one that consistently made money, and its earnings defrayed some of the costs of running other departments in which high numbers of uninsured patients strained the budget. During staff meetings, hospital administrators frequently issued reminders of the importance of retaining patients by streamlining the intake process so that women who received a positive pregnancy test at Beaumont could quickly be entered into the hospital's prenatal care. Departmental administrators were well aware of women's dissatisfaction with long delays (I was surprised and rather touched to see the genuine distress expressed by one high-ranking administrator at the issue) and had taken a number of measures in an attempt to improve patient flow, from internal studies designed to identify sources of time "leakage" and "bottlenecks" to an extensive reorganization of the clinical suites. Yet, too often, as Barry Saunders writes, the relationship between clinical space and flow of bodies was "more dynamic and resistant to planning than notions of archival management would suggest" (2010, 184).

The intransigence of the problem was driven home to me one morning in the clinic hallway when I ran into Dr. Becker, a high-level administrator who had supported my research in the department. With his urging, the department had just completed a labor- and time-intensive effort to move the low-risk prenatal clinic and its staff into the larger suite previously occupied by the family planning unit, which then took up residence in the smaller suite. It was hoped that the more spacious clinic would decrease wait times by allowing providers to "swing" between rooms, attending patients constantly as PCAs readied others for their appointment in other offices or cleaned and prepared recently vacated rooms. When I asked Dr. Becker how the move had gone, however, he smiled wryly. In an exquisite example of the use of gallows humor in medical contexts to express stress and frustration (Saunders 2010), he replied, "The move went perfectly. We moved all of the same problems we were having in the old suite right into the new one." When I pressed him, he sobered quickly, ascribing the problem of continued delays to the "culture" of the low-risk clinical practitioners (all nurse-practitioners or midwives) and their lack of sense of "time urgency," in contrast to the physician-staffed high-risk prenatal clinic, which, he claimed, "moved patients through pretty efficiently."

Since I did not conduct observation in the high-risk clinic, I am unable to comment comparatively on provider "culture" or patient experience in that environment. Much scholarship on reproduction has remarked upon the differences between doctors and midwives in their approach to clinical time management (e.g., Davis-Floyd 2004; McCourt 2013; Niles et al. 2021). It is clear that a more rapid patient "flow," while decreasing wait times for patients, is not always desirable: what an administrator might see as time efficiency may be perceived by patients as being rushed or dismissive. My observations in the low-risk clinic suggest that Dr. Becker's analysis did hold some truth, however, as we will see shortly. Yet like all practices, these temporal cultures arose amidst specific material conditions that sometimes escaped the gaze of otherwise astute observers.

One factor was the crumbling infrastructure that significantly slowed the pace of work. The obstetric department's 2016 internal time study, for example, identified technological problems and outdated hardware and software as a significant contributor to delays. I witnessed a number of occasions when a nurse or provider stalked out of her room in the middle of writing up patient notes, declaring that her computer had once again crashed and needed to be rebooted, losing a precious fifteen or twenty minutes during which she would become even more backlogged with patients. "How do they expect us to work?" exclaimed Ms. Butler, a nurse-practitioner, in exasperation to no one in particular. "How do they expect us to do our jobs if they can't even give us computers that work?" Ms. Butler was well known for her irritability, and her tirade elicited little response from others. Yet her frustration at the hospital's material conditions was widely shared; clinical staff, from administrators to receptionists, complained about the tribulations of providing care given aging computers, unreliable software for scheduling appointments in different departments, slow responses to maintenance calls, and frequent and often uncomfortable variability in the heating and cooling systems. Ms. Butler's commentary about her aging computer thus gave voice to a more widely held perception that the "system" did not adequately value their time and labor, as measured by the failure to provide resources that would allow them to perform their jobs efficiently.

Structural inequalities thus shaped conditions of care and clinical time for everyone at Beaumont. Michaela Johnson, the former discount retail worker, recalled her previous appointment to me, saying, "Well, the last one took quite a while. I think it took three to four hours. And then the computer system shut down so half the stuff that they did, they couldn't even put it in. That's frustrating. I sat here for all this time and now you're telling me [that] I have to come do this again?" Patients sometimes explicitly recognized the shared conditions of resource constraint and its effect on providers; Shanelle Tompkins, the health aide who cared for her disabled father, told me, "My visit before, I was aggravated. The system went down and I was here from ten [o'clock] and I did not leave until about two or three." Yet she immediately acknowledged, "It wasn't the doctor's fault. When I got inside the office I saw the doctor was frustrated too."

For clinical staff, resource disparities, as well as the structures of time that these material inequities produce, contributed to a sense that they were overworked, underpaid, and undervalued (at least in comparison to their counterparts at more prestigious private hospitals) (Strong 2020). Joanna, the midwife, described the physical and emotional "burnout" that ultimately led her to leave the safety net hospital system: "I would be running from patient to patient like a crazy person. And I'd finish and think, 'I haven't eaten, had a drink of water, or gone to the bathroom for my entire shift. My own health is suffering.'" Even so, she noted, "our [prenatal] visits are five minutes long because we can't give more time than that. That feels terrible, especially when I know you've been sitting outside waiting to see me for an hour and a half. And now I'm basically saying, 'Okay, you're good. Your baby's alive. Great. See you in two weeks.' That feels really terrible." In their own experiences of emotional and physical discomfort, providers illuminated how structures of clinical time and temporal governance undermined their own sense of professional integrity and professional and personal well-being.

The stress of constantly working under time pressure—what Dr. Becker referred to as "time urgency"—thus brought to the fore tensions around what Paul Brodwin (2013) calls "everyday ethics," as frontline providers found their self-perception as competent and compassionate professionals challenged by the strains of caring for patients in difficult material circumstances. Under conditions requiring that staff work faster while patients waited longer, clinical interactions often became infused with conflicts over time that played out both between staff and patients and between staff members themselves. From my position behind the reception desk, I was not infrequently witness to backstage tensions as providers questioned the reasons for patient backlog, complained about perceived patient overload, or debated who would take on a heavily pregnant walk-in patient with no history of prenatal care at Beaumont. Some providers routinely stayed late and took short or no lunches in order to accommodate patients who, they acknowledged, had likely navigated multiple other demands to their time in order to attend prenatal care. "She may be late," Dr. Silva told me, "but she's here. I don't know what it took for her to get here. And since she's here, it's my job to make sure she gets care. If I tell her to come back another day because she's late, who knows if she'll come back at all?"

Through articulations of everyday ethics, some providers tied their willingness to make time accommodations to their broader social commitments of caring for vulnerable people. Others, however, responded to time pressure by asserting control over their labor time even at the expense of patients: taking longer-than-scheduled lunch breaks, coming in late for their shifts, or refusing to see patients who arrived late. Strategies of temporal control through practices of delay and "slowdown" were both a means to resist administrative pressures to work faster and a way of asserting their status in a labor context in which they often felt unappreciated. On one occasion, after a miscommunication between two providers resulted in a new obstetric patient being left in the waiting room for almost four hours without being seen, Ms. Butler, the nurse-practitioner assigned to her care, subsequently refused to see her because it was "too late in the day for a new patient." Shocked and dismayed by this refusal, the PCAs and reception staff gathered in the hall to express their indignation. Finally, Ms. Jones, a vocal PCA, stalked angrily away, loudly declaring her sympathy with the patient: "This place needs a shake-up. Something is broken here, really broken." In refusing to see a new patient at the end of her working day, Ms. Butler asserted her agency and power in a temporal system in which she felt unappreciated and overburdened. Yet in so doing, she reproduced a medicosocial hierarchy in which patients often felt that the "system" did not care about them or their time.

The providers with whom I spoke almost universally agreed with Ms. Jones's assessment that the "system" was "broken" and served neither the well-being of the patients nor that of the providers. However, they also struggled to respond to my queries about how safety net healthcare had become, as Ms. Richards, a midwife, put it, "so dysfunctional that you can't care too much. . . . People who have to survive here all day every day because that is their job have to, in order to function, put up some kind of wall." Her comment illuminates the challenges that unforgiving clinical temporal regimes and material scarcity can pose to providers' ethics of care. Under these conditions, caring "too much" can become a liability; the unrelenting effort of trying to extend more than technical care under constant time pressure, Ms. Richards argues, hurts providers and leads to burnout and withdrawal from practice in the safety net health institutions, despite the social and political commitments that initially led many providers to work in these hospitals.

Frustrations over time that were largely rooted in broader structural inequalities were thus often displaced onto patients themselves. On one occasion, I observed an interaction during which one of the receptionists, Ms. Hayworth, realized that a woman waiting to check in was already forty minutes late for her appointment. Hospital policy was unclear on whether or not she should register the patient and, as she hesitated, a health educator cum low-level administrator leaned forward and told the woman, "You missed your appointment. You're forty minutes late. We can schedule you for another appointment on another day, but you can't be seen today." The woman frowned, obviously displeased, but did not protest. As she walked away with her new appointment written on the back of her card, he called after her, "Don't be late for that one!" Then, turning to me, he declared, "That's the problem here. Patients are in the habit of thinking they can just be seen whenever they show up, and so they miss their appointment and everyone says, 'Don't worry, just go. It's Beaumont, they'll see you.' But if we want to be like a private hospital, we have to act like one. And that means teaching women to come on time or they won't be seen. It's not the Islands here."

In his analysis, the numerous other constraints that shape patients' ability to access care "on time"—transportation difficulties, work obligations, lack of childcare, or the simple inability to obtain an appointment at times that work for their schedules—are collapsed into the facile language of "habit" that references entrenched personal and social characteristics rather than structural ones. The declaration by the administrator—himself Black—that this (US) hospital was not the Caribbean islands (where many of the patients had strong transnational ties) reveals the insidious legacy of racist colonial representations in which "natives" are, for better or for worse, less bound by the punctual mores of "civilized society," which is always coded as white (Cooper and Stoler 1997; Nanni 2017). In singling out patient "habits," rather than the material or temporal factors that constrain both patients and providers, as the reason that Beaumont did not operate like the private hospitals that were inevitably held up as the gold standard of healthcare, this administrator articulated the same racial sentiments that have long animated colonial and imperialist logic; if patients could only be taught to arrive on time, goes this thinking, Beaumont too would be like the private hospitals to which it aspired. Through such displacements, the effects of structural inequalities are individualized and blamed on the temporal cultures of pregnant patients themselves, reproducing wider discourses in which the poor are seen as responsible for their own condition and obfuscating their roots in broader and long-standing racial injustices.

Conclusion

Attention to clinical time sharply underscores how temporal regimes and forms of temporal governance reflect and reproduce broader racial and class inequalities, negatively shaping healthcare encounters for patients and providers. These temporal structures are consequential: time-pressured providers are more likely to misdiagnose or overlook signs of chronic or emergent high-risk conditions, make prescription errors, or make other preventable—and potentially dangerous—mistakes. For patients, chronic delays are experienced as a lack of care and respect for their time and persons that can make accessing prenatal care an aggravating or even hostile undertaking, deterring women from attending regular prenatal care or follow-up consultations for high-risk conditions. Perceptions of provider stress and haste can also make patients uncertain about whether to "burden" a provider with their concerns, with potentially deleterious consequences for their health.

Clinical time is thus a key vector through which racialized patient populations, as well as the medical staff who work in racialized systems of public healthcare, encounter the lesser value assigned to their time, bodies, and labor. In the next and final chapter, we will examine how movements for temporal justice are attempting to dismantle these entrenched hierarchies by calling for a broader politics of care that is enacted not only between individuals, but in social policy as well.

4

Cosmologies of Care

Temporal Justice and the Politics of Value

On a late summer day toward the end of my fieldwork, I ran into Yvonne Auguste, a Haitian home health aide then seven months pregnant with her fourth child, pushing her sixteen-month-old son in a stroller outside the WIC office at Beaumont Hospital. During our interview some months prior, she had told me about her efforts to find an apartment. Her current living situation was deeply unsatisfactory: she, her husband, and their three children rented a single bedroom in a house owned by another Haitian migrant. Her landlady did not allow her to use the kitchen or to prepare food in her bedroom, forcing the family to choose between buying every meal out or eating prepackaged dry goods in their room. I had thought about her often in the months since, and I inquired hopefully about her search. Yvonne shook her head sadly, expressing incredulity at the cost and the competition for even poor-quality apartments. For now, this meant that her family of soon-to-be six would have to continue to live in their single-room quarters.

At my expression of dismay, Yvonne told me that she had been hoping to see me as she had been having trouble at work. Her supervisor had assigned her a new case, but it was a difficult one, "a hard patient," as Yvonne put it, requiring constant bending and lifting, which were difficult at her advanced state of pregnancy. She didn't know why she had been assigned to this case, particularly since she had provided her supervisor with a doctor's note confirming her pregnancy and expected due date. But when she asked to be transferred to a "lighter" case, her supervisor responded that she was unable to reassign her and, moreover, that she "could not deal" with Yvonne's repeated requests for a transfer.

With few other options, Yvonne continued to do the best she could with her client. Two weeks prior to our conversation, however, her client's son had dropped by for a visit during her shift. Seeing Yvonne, he had expressed shock at her heavily pregnant state and her obvious difficulty when moving and bathing his father. He called Yvonne's supervisor, complaining that they had sent a pregnant home health aide who was unable to provide proper care. At this, according to Yvonne, the supervisor demurred, exclaiming, "She's not pregnant, she's just fat!"

Yvonne paused in her narration, repeating incredulously, "She said that! She said I was fat! She lied! There's no respect. She has to give people respect!" Pulling out a crumpled copy of the flyer describing the Pregnant Workers Fairness Act that I distributed during my informational presentations, she told me that she had called 311 (New York City's general telephone line for non-emergency services and information about city government programs) as the flyer instructed but that no one had called her back. Now, she told me, she wanted my help in lodging a complaint against her supervisor.

The Pregnant Workers Fairness Act and the Paid Safe and Sick Leave Act reshaped the policy landscape in New York City by connecting issues of reproduction and care to broader movements for rights and social justice. No longer could an employer's refusal to make reasonable work accommodations for pregnant employees or to allow eligible employees paid time off for medical or care reasons be dismissed as simply disrespectful or unpleasant behavior that the worker had to endure. It was now a violation of their rights as working pregnant people that could be remedied through appeals to the state.

Such legislation is an essential step in realizing social change. Yet research has shown that the concept of rights is often at odds with the interpretive frameworks used by the desired beneficiaries of these laws, potentially limiting their ability or willingness to use legal protections to challenge existing power relations (Hodgson 2011; Merry 2009; Ticktin 2011). To my knowledge, Yvonne was the only one of my study participants to attempt to lodge a formal complaint under this new legislation, and her efforts illuminate some of the difficulties facing workers hoping to claim their newly instated rights. As we will see, official channels of adjudication require complainants to narrate events within a language of rights that did not always map neatly onto women's own understanding of labor relations as unfolding within relations of care.

A growing body of anthropological research has taken care as its central ethnographic and analytic focus, showing that it can be a moral practice that produces and reinforces human and more-than-human social bonds (Kleinman 2009; Mol 2008), but also showing that institutions and individuals can reproduce relations of neglect and even violence under the guise of providing care (Biehl 2012; Mulla 2014; Stevenson 2014; Ticktin 2011). Such analyses expand the definition of care, viewing it as a set of practices and vital politics that connect not only individuals as members of kin groups and communities, but also states to citizen-subjects. If care is a "social and emotional practice that . . . entails the capacity to make, shape, and be made by social bonds" (Alber and Drotbohm 2015, 2), states and nations are also engaged in practices of caring (or not) for their subjects through forms of institutional care as well as through policies and practices that "hail" individuals and communities as part of a larger social and political body politic (Briggs and Mantini-Briggs 2016; Lewis 2017).

This chapter elaborates this cosmology of care by considering its place as a primary idiom through which pregnant workers evaluated workplace relationships and conditions, illuminating the disconnect between workers' interpretations of care as a private matter negotiated between individuals and the universal language of rights promoted in legislation like the Pregnant Workers Fairness Act. By contrast, as policy action around New York's Paid Family Leave Act (PFLA) highlights, advocates for temporal justice argue that time to care is a right: a caring state protects *all* working people's ability to engage in care work without fear of economic disaster. In so doing, they also work to symbolically and materially re-value the work of care.

Rights Talk and the Pregnant Workers Fairness Act

Yvonne and I walked out of the noisy building that housed the WIC office into the bright sunshine outside. I dialed 311, putting my phone on speaker so that we could both hear, and was immediately presented with a menu of options, all in English, listing different city services and departments. Uncertain which department would handle her complaint, I selected the option to speak to a representative and was connected surprisingly quickly. Upon hearing that I was calling on behalf of someone who wished to file a pregnancy discrimination claim, the representative directed me, incorrectly as it turns out, to the Labor Relations Department. At the Labor Relations Department, the agent informed us that alleged pregnancy discrimination was handled by the city's Commission on Human Rights and provided us with the correct telephone number (which was omitted in all the city-produced literature about the Pregnant Workers Fairness Act).

At the Human Rights Commission, a woman clearly and patiently explained the multi-step process. Upon receiving notification that Yvonne intended to file a complaint, the commission would send a paper form to her home address. This form needed to be filled out with specific information about the basis for her complaint, including dates and the nature of the infraction, and returned to the commission. After the commission received her written form, it would begin investigations to establish whether there were grounds for her case, and a determination would be made approximately four weeks later.

Given the often labyrinthine call menus that many institutions force callers to navigate before connecting them to a live representative, I was impressed by the relative ease of reaching an agent and her clear explanation of the process. But when I looked at Yvonne, her face was drawn tight in disappointment, and I realized that she had imagined a more rapid process and immediate response to her troubles. Now, sensing that the interaction was drawing to a close, she leaned close to my phone to exclaim loudly, "She called me fat! That's not right. That's why I want to complain to you. There's no respect!"

At this pronouncement, the woman on the other end of the telephone line paused, clearly at a loss for how to respond. After a moment of silence, she quickly returned to the official script. Reframing Yvonne's indignation as a question of process, she reiterated that Yvonne needed to document all the information pertaining to her claim on the official form to lodge a formal complaint. With a resigned sigh, Yvonne provided the representative with a mailing address, and I offered to help her to fill out the form when it arrived. We both expressed hope that she would soon have luck in her apartment search and in being transferred to a more appropriate case. After talking for a few more minutes, we hugged each other goodbye, with Yvonne promising to contact me if she needed help to continue with her pregnancy discrimination complaint.

Yvonne's brief encounter with the Commission on Human Rights reveals a number of obstacles to those workers who might wish to claim their newly defined rights. First, pregnant workers must be aware that they are legally accorded certain protections during pregnancy. Yet time and again, I found that women were unaware of these policies, despite a concerted effort by the city to publicize them through billboards and flyers. Although employers are required by law to display information about workers' rights in a public shared space, only two of the fifty-five women I interviewed had any recollection of having seen these materials. In some cases, employers likely failed to make this information publicly available to their employees, a well-documented breach of legal requirements (A Better Balance 2021b). In others, as some women noted, signage may have been posted in break rooms or on bulletin boards. However, no supervisor had ever drawn their attention to them or discussed their import—an important factor in a mobile population of workers with large numbers of non-proficient English speakers. Moreover, many categories of service laborers, such as home-based caregivers and domestic workers, are based primarily within "private" spaces with

An electronic billboard in New York City's subway system seeks to promote awareness of pregnant workers' rights. Photograph by the author.

few public shared areas in which they might encounter this information. As Lucia Germaine, the home health aide, observed, "There's really nowhere to post [the material]. I never go to the agency. My supervisor just calls me when my cases change, and I go there [to the client's house], so that's probably why I haven't seen them."

With little information about legal protections, women drew on previous experience and alternative circulations of knowledge to make decisions about navigating future reproductive and labor time. During interviews, I was continually struck by how few of my interlocutors had inquired about their company's policies on pregnancy accommodations or paid parental leave, even though some were in late stages of pregnancy by the time we spoke. Some simply assumed that no such policies or benefits existed. Others told me frankly that they did not initiate discussions about accommodations because they feared provoking hostility from their supervisors. Ayesha Thomas, the assistant manager at a fast-food restaurant who had recently suffered a miscarriage, declared, "I didn't even bother asking [about leaves]. There was one girl before me who got pregnant, and they just made things so difficult for her that she ended up quitting. I just figure, I'll work till things get bad and then I'll leave." Some of the women also expressed fear that supervisors would (illegally) retaliate against workers who requested pregnancy accommodations through strategies of temporal control, such as withholding hours or scheduling women to undesirable cases or shifts, that essentially force workers out of their jobs (Silver-Greenberg and Kitroeff 2018). Undocumented workers felt their lack of power particularly acutely, despite also being covered by the new legislation. Tammy Greene, a thirty-eight-year-old Trinidadian food-service worker at a popular buffet restaurant around the corner from Beaumont Hospital, told me,

> They tell you, "Shut up, or we will not pay you." . . . I think people think you don't know what your rights are, or you don't have the documents in the country so you're afraid to speak out. Because even when minimum wages was raised, they still paid me only four dollars an hour. . . . Nobody

pays the laws no mind because we don't pay them [the laws] no mind. So they do what they want and we are too afraid to do anything.

As Tammy and Ayesha make clear, in addition to being aware of their legal rights, workers must also believe that they have a reasonable chance of success in pursuing their claims. Most of the women I interviewed, however, expressed the opinion that the Pregnant Workers Fairness Act would be unlikely to have a positive effect in their own workplace; with few, if any, models of successful change, lodging a formal complaint with the city appeared to them to be, at best, unlikely to succeed and, at worst, likely to simply escalate hostilities at work. Given these anticipated outcomes, they relied on the hope that their good relations with supervisors and co-workers would help them to reconcile potential conflicts—while quietly preparing to leave their jobs should working conditions become too inhospitable. This is not unusual: studies have shown that nearly one in four working pregnant people have considered leaving their place of employment due to pregnancy discrimination or employer failures to extend pregnancy-related accommodations (Gitis, Sprick, and Schweer 2022).

The second set of obstacles are the linguistic and structural capacities assumed by the complaint process, despite the attempts by the law's authors to make its reach as broad as possible. The automated message that first greets callers to New York City's 311 line is in English. Although callers can then select from a variety of languages, they must not be put off by the lengthy initial message detailing instructions to call 911 for emergencies as well as information about daily parking regulations. Once connected to a representative in their preferred language, they must be able to succinctly explain their situation, be connected to the appropriate department (Human Rights, not Labor Relations), and understand the process required to file a formal complaint. In addition, the requirement that complainants receive a mailed form at their "home address" assumes a stable address where they can access mail. Yet this is far from certain. While rental and housing prices in densely populated New

York have always ranked among the highest in the country, the pressure on housing has dramatically increased since the Great Recession in 2008 (and reached unprecedented heights following the COVID-19 pandemic starting in 2020). In the years following the Great Recession, the longstanding dearth of affordable housing, the loss of jobs and breadwinners, and low and stagnant wages combined to produce a worsening crisis for low-income families, despite the strong tenant protections for which New York City is known. During my fieldwork in 2015, fifty-eight thousand people applied to just 105 affordable homes in New York City (Desmond 2016). Although popular perceptions of homelessness usually call up stereotypes of single men with substance abuse or mental health conditions, up to two-thirds of those in the city's shelter system are families with children, and one in three of those families have some type of income (Carp 2022). Many of those with income are employed in the low-wage service sector in home care, retail, or fast food (Gay 2017). Essentially invisible to the public eye, these families may live precariously for years, when an unforeseen crisis such as illness or the loss of a job forces them out of their homes. Most seek shelter first in the homes of friends and relatives, only entering the city's notoriously chaotic and overcrowded shelter system, where shelter policies may separate fathers from families or even parents from children, as a last resort.

Although none of the women who participated in this research explicitly described themselves as "homeless" or "unstably housed," it was not uncommon for my interlocutors to describe movements between the apartments of partners, family members, and various rented rooms with a frequency that would make it difficult to reliably receive postal mail. This appeared to be particularly true for immigrant women. Yvonne and her family, for example, rented a room in a house owned by a more established Haitian migrant, whose practice of illegally subdividing rooms for families in need had resulted in an occupancy rate far above that permitted by the city. Fearing detection, her landlady had forbidden any of her tenants to list the house as their mailing address; the address that Yvonne provided was in fact the mailing address of a friend. Yvonne assured me that her friend would surely contact her upon receiving any mail, although she admitted that this process could occasionally take some time. But this arrangement was a fragile one that could collapse if her friend's living situation were to change or if the friendship were to lapse. The intricate arrangements that Yvonne describes thus highlight the problematic assumption of housing stability that are embedded in the commission's apparently simple requirement of receiving a paper form.

Finally, and perhaps most consequentially, women had to perceive a negative workplace interaction as illegal or a "rights violation," rather than simply the actions of an inconsiderate supervisor, and know how to make their complaint legible as such to adjudicating bodies. As scholars have observed, human rights frameworks have become the dominant approach to social justice (Burrell 2010; Hodgson 2011; Merry 2009; Ticktin 2011). Indeed, it is notable that the adjudication procedures for the Pregnant Workers Fairness Act are handled by the city's Commission on Human Rights rather than by its Department of Consumer and Worker Protection, which investigates violations of the city's Paid Safe and Sick Leave Act and Fair Workweek Law. As this division of jurisdiction makes clear, pregnant workers become a protected class with claims rooted in human rights rather than labor law alone (Merry 2006, 2009).

Human rights, as defined by the United Nations Human Rights Commission, are those "inalienable rights" inherent to all people, ranging from the right to life to rights to food, housing, and education, which the state is obligated to protect.[1] The logic of human rights, as Miriam Ticktin argues in her critique of the politics of care in French humanitarian organizations, requires the production of "universal humanity" in which "suffering [is] configured as a particular biological form with affective resonance—enough to compel moral action" (2011, 13). In New York City, the website of the Human Rights Commission notes that the city's human rights law is one of the most comprehensive in the country, prohibiting "discrimination in employment, housing, and public accommodations based on race, color, religion/creed, age, national origin, immigration or citizenship status, gender (including sexual harassment), gender identity, sexual orientation, disability, pregnancy, marital status, and partnership status."[2]

In defining pregnancy discrimination as a form of gender discrimination, already protected under the city's human rights law, the Pregnant Workers Fairness Act dramatically reshaped the landscape of rights for pregnant workers in New York City. Prior to its passage, under the federal Pregnancy Discrimination Act, people who brought pregnancy-related labor complaints against employers were required to prove that their pregnancy constituted a temporary disability (since disability is a protected category) and that they were treated differently than nonpregnant workers with similar disabilities. Given this burden of proof, claims by people with routine or uncomplicated pregnancies were often rejected. By contrast, the Pregnant Workers Fairness Act encompasses a broad definition of violations, from disparate treatment of pregnant workers and pregnancy-related harassment to failure to provide reasonable accommodations, pointing out that even "subtle and patronizing" forms of discrimination "push pregnant individuals out of the job market, disrupt earnings, and hamper economic advancement" (New York City Commission on Human Rights 2021, 4).

For pregnant workers, lodging a successful complaint thus requires the ability to narrate lived experience within the established frameworks and discourses of rights. Practices of "translation" (Merry 2006) are crucial to making violence and suffering legible as human rights violations: intimate partner violence and political persecution, for example, may qualify while poverty and immiseration do not. The repeated statement by the otherwise helpful person at the commission that Yvonne should "document all relevant information" presumes that what constitutes evidence is simply a natural or obvious reiteration of "the facts." Yet it is not always clear which facts are relevant. To me, the most compelling fact was the refusal of Yvonne's supervisor to transfer her to an appropriate case, leaving her with the choice to quit and lose badly needed income or to remain on a job that required intense physical labor during the last months of her pregnancy. Yvonne, however, appeared to take this denial of "reasonable accommodations" as a frustrating but not unprecedented supervisory decision. Rather, what brought her to lodge a complaint was her sense of moral injury when her supervisor attributed her slow movements and bodily appearance to obesity rather than pregnancy. For her, the most important fact was her perception of disrespect caused by her supervisor's false claims about her pregnancy status.

Our contrasting perspectives highlight the ambiguities and ambivalences involved in constructing a human rights complaint. Given New York City's broad definition of pregnancy discrimination, it is possible that the comments of Yvonne's supervisor could fall under the category of pregnancy-based harassment, which includes negative comments and "jokes" about a pregnant person. Yvonne herself, as her response made clear, interpreted this interaction as deeply insulting and demeaning. (Indeed, she was so angry when we spoke that she had no interest in speculating on her supervisor's motivations, although I asked her several times. It was only in retrospect that I wondered whether perhaps her supervisor thought that she was protecting Yvonne by hiding the fact of her pregnancy from her client and his family.) For her, a complaint constructed around a denial of accommodations would fail to capture the primary reason for her sense of injustice. Regardless, I suspected that the claim of pregnancy-based harassment would be far more difficult to substantiate, and I worried that Yvonne would not find a receptive audience for her complaint. These issues of translation are significant, since low-wage workers often have little experience in these areas and, as Alana Glaser (2020) finds in her ethnography of organizing among in-home care workers in New York City, workers' groups may see themselves as spaces of solidarity and bonding rather than as forums to instruct workers about the rhetorical and practical strategies to successfully file complaints about labor violations.

Unfortunately, I do not know the conclusion of this story. I did not hear from Yvonne again and concluded fieldwork at Beaumont shortly after this encounter took place. When I tried to contact her a month or so later to find out whether she had received the form and whether she needed help to file her complaint, I discovered that her cell phone, the only permanent phone number for her as for many of the women in my study, had been disconnected.

Caring and Not Caring: Personalist Interpretive Frameworks

If policy initiatives intended to establish and protect pregnant workers are to positively affect the lives of their target constituency, local grievances must be re-crafted as human rights violations. Yet, as Yvonne's situation underscores, experiences of humiliation or indignation are not "naturally" understood within established discourses of rights. Resources to help workers to construct and lodge rights complaints exist: in New York City, legal advocacy organizations like A Better Balance as well as various unions offer support and free legal advice. For workers to even begin this process, however, requires that they have already conceptualized their grievances as injustices from which the state should protect them rather than seeing them as interpersonal tensions that remain within the "private" realm of employer-employee relationships (Levitsky 2008; Merry 2009).

This is no small shift. In my interviews, I found that participants never framed employers' refusals to make accommodations for their pregnancies as a violation of their *rights*. Rather, they described these actions within a personalized discourse of care. In sectors such as home health care (Buch 2018; Coe 2019), childcare (Glaser 2020), and domestic work (Rosenbaum 2017), anthropologists have shown how the conditions of low-wage care work encourage workers to view employer-employee interactions in terms of personal rather than contractual relations. According to sociologist Judith Rollins (1985), this dynamic is rooted in the legacies of the "master-slave" interaction in domestic and care work, in which subordinates are cast as "one of the family" in ways that often enable and legitimate labor exploitation (see also Glenn 1992). For example, the willingness of a child's caregiver to repeatedly stay beyond agreed-upon hours at short notice may be interpreted by both worker and employee as an expression of love and care that may not demand additional monetary compensation. The mutual framing of the caregiver as "like family," whose members are expected to perform care work for each other for free, serves to obscure and legitimize situations of labor exploitation. Personalist frameworks may also shape responses to conflict by encouraging workers to interpret injustices through the interpersonal language of humiliation and disrespect, drawing on "personal judgments of their employers, in lieu of formal workplace grievances, to confront the inequities of their work arrangements" (Glaser 2020, 196; see also Coe 2019).

While this literature locates personalism within the intimate spaces of long-term care work, my research reveals the prevalence of this interpretive framework even in those short-term and non-care-related working arrangements that might otherwise be expected to adhere to a more contractual interpretation of labor relationships. Given the "churn" of low-wage workers through different forms of service labor (Boushey 2016), my findings suggest that as workers move from home health care to retail to food service and back again, personalist interpretive frameworks circulate with them. As we will see in the following vignettes, it is in the language of care, rather than rights and contracts, that pregnant service workers interpreted work conditions and workplace interactions.

Discourses of Caring in Employer-Employee Relations

Until recently, Nicola Smith had worked as a baby nurse for a family in an area of Brooklyn where the spacious brick row houses were owned mostly by large traditional Orthodox Jewish families. Contracted to work for the family for six months for seventy-five dollars a day, she not only took care of the newborn baby who was her official charge, but also the three other children under five years of age who needed constant attention and supervision. "I really took care of them," she told me during our interview at the clinic. "And I thought that that meant something to them." The crisis, as she related it, came during Passover, one of the most sacred holidays in the Jewish calendar. In the days leading up to this religious event, observant Jews clean their homes of any leavened bread in a rite that recalls their biblical exodus from Egypt. In traditional Orthodox homes, women rid their kitchens of bread, cereal, pasta, rice, oats, beans, and any processed foods that might contain leaven.

For live-in caregivers like Nicola, whose contract stipulated that her low daily wages must be supplemented by free room and board, holidays such as Passover pose a problem. When she discovered that her clients planned to take their older children to celebrate the holiday with relatives for a few days, Nicola secured assurances that they would purchase ritually permissible foods for her to cook for herself while she remained with her newborn charge. But as the family was hurrying out the door, she was told that no food had been purchased. For Nicola, this oversight, intentional or not, was the last straw in a working relationship that she already felt was bordering on the exploitative. She declared to me, "I told them, 'I cared for you, I cared for your family, and I thought that you would care for me too, but that's not the case. You know that I am pregnant, you know that I need to eat, and I thought you would care about me and my child, but you don't." And then, she told me, she walked out the door, ignoring their entreaties to stay. "I just left. I was hungry, I had to eat. And my baby comes first. I told them, 'This is my baby, and I thought you would care for my baby like I cared for yours. But now I have to take care of myself.'"

In Nicola's narrative, claims of harm were made not through reference to her client's breach of contract but rather in the language of personal relationships. Caught between labor time and gestational time, she felt that the family's failure to consider her need for food while she was pregnant and "on the clock" was a material instantiation of their lack of care. In asserting her unmet expectations of reciprocity—"I thought you would care for my baby like I cared for yours"—she framed her relationship to her client in interpersonal terms, as two structurally similar women who relied on each other for their children's well-being. From Nicola's perspective, her care-full attention to her employer's children went beyond the simple exchange of payment for (affective) labor; it was a gift that obliged the recipient to reciprocate in kind (Mauss [1925] 1954). Her employer's failure to provide food could not therefore be dismissed as a minor oversight; for her, it was a devastating lapse in a gendered temporal cycle of reciprocal care for pregnant and birthing bodies. Profoundly disillusioned, she asserted her own worth through leaving to "take care of myself."

But personalist interpretive frameworks were not expressed only by those women working in "intimate" domestic settings. Michaela Johnson, the former retail worker now employed at a call center, concluded her interview by telling me with no small amount of satisfaction that her supervisors at the retail store had approached her to work for them again now that her morning sickness had passed and she felt stronger. "But," she told me, "I won't do it. I was a good worker, but they threw me to the wolves.... I just would rather be homeless before I work for a place that could care less about me and my child's health. I can get another job, but my child is my child." In this temporally delayed cycle of reciprocity, Michaela expected that her history of hard work and commitment to the company would be recognized through support and accommodation during the time-limited period of her pregnancy. When this was not forthcoming, she describes her sense of betrayal not as a denial of rights but as an absence of care.

Personalism shapes interpretations of more positively valenced labor relations as well. When I asked Michaela about her current working conditions at the call center, she declared,

> They take good care of me over there. The supervisor is like, "All right, I know she's pregnant." The other people can't be snacking around, but she makes sure, "All right, take your break early if you need to. Get water if you need to." Everyone in there is like, "What do you need? Did you eat?" They're more like mommies to me over there.

For Michaela, care is made evident in every encounter in her new workplace, from queries about her well-being to affirmations of her need for more frequent food and water breaks given her pregnant state. Interpreted through a gendered metaphor of kin ties ("they're like mommies to me"), workplace accommodations become acts of care that reflect the nurturance and intimacy expected of relations between mothers and daughters.

Personalism, Time, and Expectations of Care

Personalist interpretations of labor relations thus appear to flourish in environments where workers are unaware of the existence of either state or corporate policy and where benefits and accommodations are seen as private negotiations between employer and employee. When expectations of reciprocal care are upheld, personalism can make a workplace feel familial; through affective and relational practices of care, supervisors and co-workers become "like kin." When they are not, workers may feel betrayed and vulnerable. Shanelle Phillips, an aide at a nursing home pregnant with her first child, told me with palpable anger that her supervisor had refused her requests to be assigned to more mobile patients with less need for heavy lifting. "I feel like she doesn't care about me," she said. "I'm pregnant and trying to work, and she doesn't even care. I thought she would [care] because I knew her before—she even used to come to my salon when I was still doing hair—but she doesn't." For Shanelle, her intimate relationship with the woman who later became her supervisor led her to expect that she would receive flexibility and accommodation during her pregnancy, resulting in disillusionment when this did not materialize.

In the context of service work, personalism and unspoken assumptions of care and intimacy may contribute to women's reluctance to preemptively discuss workplace policy or future accommodations with employers and supervisors. Analyzing practices of care in Italy, Andrea Muehlebach points to the difference between pacts, which are rooted in notions of gratitude and reciprocity, and contracts, which have a "temporal stability and predictability ... made possible by the presence of a mediating party, the state, which acts as an enforcing power between contracting parties. Through contract, futurity is written into the very structure of the present" (2012, 46). Guaranteed by the state, contracts allow both parties the ability to predict, with near confidence, how the future of their relationship will play out. By contrast, pacts are based on expectations of trust and intimacy that "largely proceed by way of what goes without saying" (Berlant 2011, 686). The often unspoken nature of pacts introduces temporal uncertainty and economic and emotional instability into the lives of workers, since the exact benefits that they may receive in the future may be left unspoken and workers may have no recourse if their expectations are not met.

Personalism has other implications as well. In my interviews, I found that a personalist interpretation of labor relations not only made it less likely that pregnant workers would see failures to provide accommodations as violations of their *own* rights. It also limited their willingness to see such accommodations as the right of *all* pregnant workers. Faced with disappointments, the women I spoke with echoed Michaela Johnson's sentiment, protesting failures of care by describing themselves as "good workers" who were deserving of better treatment. But this "vocabulary of virtue" (Macdonald and Merrill 2002) is quite different from a logic of rights that would assert that *all* pregnant workers deserved the same treatment, regardless of their work ethic or commitment to their jobs. Discourses of deservingness, as Sarah Willen (2012) argues in the context of healthcare access for immigrants to the United States, are the "flip side" of rights; whereas claims to rights are made in juridical language that presumes universality and equality, discourses around moral deservingness are context-dependent, relational, and conditional upon presumed or actual characteristics of the individual or group. But what constitutes a "good worker"? Is it simply someone who clocks in and out on time? Someone who provides the company additional (unpaid) labor by coming in early and staying late? Someone who demonstrates company loyalty by years on the job? Who not only performs the required tasks but does so with enthusiasm and cheerfulness? While apparently self-explanatory, the concept of the good worker is a nebulous and free-floating category that is meaningful only in relation to its opposite: the "bad worker." For employers, "good workers" are often those who make themselves available whenever needed. Those who have health and caregiving commitments that make them less readily available or "flexible" are often, in the eyes of the company, less reliable and committed employees (Golden, Medved, and Andaya 2023). Requests for maternity leave, time off for prenatal care, or pregnancy accommodations can thus compromise an employee's status as a "good worker" (Kitroeff and Silver-Greenberg 2019).

Given women's disproportionate representation in service work as well as their biological and social involvement in childbearing and child rearing, reliance on personalism and claims to virtue as a guarantee of labor protections has profoundly gendered impacts. Yet it has broader repercussions as well, since for whom is it possible to always be the ideal "good worker," if injury, chronic illness, pregnancy, family obligations, or caregiving responsibilities can potentially jeopardize this status? By encouraging workers to interpret accommodations as reciprocal care for virtuous and deserving workers, personalistic interpretations of labor relations frame denials as a reflection of interpersonal dynamics that require interpersonal responses, such as quitting or expressions of anger and resentment, rather than formal mitigation processes. It is these concerns that laws like the Pregnant Workers Fairness Act and New York State's Paid Family Leave Act sought to address.

New York's Paid Family Leave Act: Temporal Justice and the Politics of Value

It was a dreary November day in 2015 as I hurried toward the office in midtown Manhattan. Inside a nondescript beige conference room, a local advocacy organization was hosting a press conference to lobby for the passage of the PFLA, which was signed into law in April of the following year. Bolstered by distinguished representatives from medical, university, and advocacy organizations, as well as elected officials, speakers argued for the crucial role of the state in guaranteeing all working people time to care. They described the uneven effects of a system in which, at the time, only about 16 percent of American workers received employer-provided paid family leave (Miller and Tankersley 2019). Those in the state of New York (along with four other states and Puerto Rico) could draw upon Temporary Disability Insurance, a state program to provide short-term support to workers debilitated by a non-occupational injury or sickness, to support themselves during an unpaid leave following the birth of a child. Speakers argued, however, that Temporary Disability Insurance was both conceptually and materially inadequate as a substitute for universal paid family leave. First, they noted that pregnancy and birth are not disabilities and should not be treated as such. Second, they pointed out that weekly payments of $169 through Temporary Disability Insurance—an amount that had not risen for many years—did not provide enough to survive in one of the most expensive cities in the world. A panel of doctors then followed, describing the positive effects of paid family leave on postpartum and neonatal health, as well as its benefits for the emotional well-being of the caregivers of sick and elderly relatives.

After the expert panel concluded, the moderator opened the floor to questions and comments. Immediately, a young Black woman in her late twenties raised her hand. Introducing herself as Cintia Baron, she described her experiences of pregnancy and birth during her former employment as a home health aide. Without paid sick leave, and making only minimum wage, she had worked throughout her pregnancy. After she gave birth, she could afford to take only two weeks off work before returning. "I was still bleeding!" she recalled emphatically. "I was still bleeding, and I was lifting and carrying bedridden patients." Struggling with the physical and emotional effects of returning to work when still physically depleted from the birth, she quickly spiraled into postpartum

Advocacy materials at a 2015 lobbying event for New York's Paid Family Leave Act. Photograph by the author.

depression. After being recruited to work as an organizer with her local union, she concluded, she was in a much better place. Yet had she had access to paid leave after giving birth, she could have avoided slipping into an economically and emotionally desperate situation in the first place. Given her experience, she felt that it was her duty to speak out in the hope of helping the thousands of other women in similar situations.

Struck by her narrative, I took advantage of a chance encounter in the hallway after the press conference to ask whether we could talk in more detail. Several weeks later, we met at a restaurant near her union office and Cintia began her story again, filling in many details omitted in her short testimony during the lobbying event. She had come to the United States from Belize as a seventeen-year-old and met her soon-to-be husband when she was just eighteen, still undocumented and working "under the table" in a tax accountant's office. When she discovered that she was pregnant, he proposed. Several years later, after finally obtaining a green card, which ensured her legal residency, Cintia started working in home health care. She worked with two agencies, making about $25,000 a year, with which she supported her mother, two young brothers, and her child. Six months into her new position, she discovered that she was once again pregnant. At the time, she had only one permanent client with whom she worked twelve-hour shifts three days a week. Struggling to pay the bills, she picked up "replacements"— last-minute coverage for other home health aides who called out from a shift—and juggled three to four clients a week. Doing replacement work was emotionally and physically exhausting; Cintia was constantly encountering new families, expectations, and issues with each replacement. She commuted between cases by bus and by subway, sometimes spending several unpaid hours each day traveling from one case to another. Her one permanent client was frequently in and out of hospital; when he was hospitalized, her steady income stopped and Cintia started calling the agencies for any replacement she could get, hoping to stave off financial crisis. She received food stamps during this time, which helped, although she never qualified for welfare assistance. Having always held out legal status as a panacea for her economic difficulties, Cintia was shocked at the few benefits and lack of support even for US citizens and legal residents. "This is how they treat their own?" she recalled wondering. "Who will I turn to? There is no support. Lots of women have no support."

Cintia asked her supervisor whether she could take leave two weeks before her due date and file for Temporary Disability Insurance. It wasn't a lot, but it was something. After her son was born, however, she realized that she was not receiving the expected paychecks. She called her supervisor and the human resources office at the agency only to be informed that the necessary paperwork had never been filed to allow her to receive her promised benefits. On further investigation, Cintia discovered that her agency was supposed to have provided her with the forms to submit medical documentation confirming the pregnancy, the expected date of delivery, and the medical rationale for leave. Neither she nor her doctor had ever received this material—an oversight that Cintia suspected was deliberate after later hearing similar stories from other women at the same agency. By this time, Cintia was in dire financial straits. Unable to wait for her paperwork to be processed, and against the advice of her doctor, she returned to work. "My supervisor and the agency said it was my choice when to return to work, but what choice did I have?" she asked me rhetorically. "I had food stamps so we wouldn't starve, but who would pay the lights?"

Physically and emotionally exhausted, she fell into a postpartum depression. Her mother, who struggled with her own mental health issues, was the primary caregiver for her young son. This arrangement worried Cintia, but she couldn't afford to pay for childcare. Her hours shifted constantly depending on her caseload, and despite her effort to find replacement cases, there were some weeks when she worked only twenty hours, sending her into a panic about the impossibility of paying for rent, food, and utilities with a weekly budget of only two hundred dollars. Meanwhile, her wildly erratic number of hours meant that she and her family constantly moved in and out of eligibility for Medicaid health coverage. Home life became an additional source of stress as Cintia and her husband sank into debt. After they parted acrimoniously, she developed migraine headaches, which she attributed to anxiety and economic worries, and her depression worsened.

Just when Cintia felt that she could not go on, she received some much-needed good news. Six months prior to our interview, the union organizer for her home health agency had put her name forward for an available position. As a union employee, Cintia enjoyed healthcare, better pay, and benefits for herself and her children. She reported feeling much happier and was starting to get back on her feet financially. She also stopped taking her antidepressants, a fact of which she was very proud. She gleefully described her encounter with her doctor at a recent appointment during which she told him that she was feeling happy and stable. He asked, "So, is the medicine working?," to which she responded, "No, but the finance is!"

Not for nothing had the union asked Cintia to speak as an advocate for paid family leave; she was a compelling narrator of her own experience and a skilled translator between the realms of policy and local experience. Drawing on her "double consciousness" (Merry 2006) as a former home health aide and current union organizer, Cintia called attention to the lack of social value attached to her reproductive time to care for herself and her dependents as opposed to her "productive" labor in caring for other families. In so doing, she starkly illuminated the urgent need for statewide paid family leave by making visible how social inequalities and structural violence, such as poverty, temporal precarity, and lack of labor protections, manifest as mental and bodily distress (Holmes 2013; Scheper-Hughes 1993). Against strong American tendencies to individualize and medicalize suffering (by treating her depression with pharmaceuticals, for example), Cintia insisted on contextualizing her experience within a wider structure of inequity that required transformative social action.

For advocates and supporters, New York's PFLA represented a historically significant effort to shift both legislation and public opinion about the social necessity of state-supported time to care. Arguing that no family should have to choose between economic survival and caring for dependents, advocates constantly reiterated the fact that *everyone* receives or gives care at some point over their life course. Calling attention to the fact that the groups made most vulnerable by the lack of state protections are those already marginalized through other durable inequalities of gender, race, class, and documentation status, supporters of the act directly connected the right to reproductive time to social justice. In so doing, they pointed to the urgency of temporal justice and a new politics of value.

Advocating for Paid Family Leave: Re-Valuing Reproductive Time

From the beginning, advocates for the act were aware of the necessity of challenging entrenched cultural beliefs that frame the material and physical costs of caregiving as responsibilities of the family rather than the state (Levitsky 2008). In the months leading up to the 2016 vote, advocates told me, polling had indicated broad support from younger respondents, particularly women. However, older men, particularly those who self-identified as white, viewed it as irrelevant to their own lives, even socially unnecessary, and objected to paying the modest one dollar per week mandatory payroll contribution for something from which they expected no personal benefit. Of course, people are constantly taxed for social projects for which they receive no direct benefit, such as contributions to public schools for households with no children or to fund wars that the taxpayer does not support. Yet this resistance revealed widespread and mistaken assumptions about both the scope of the law (that it only covered parents of newborns) and the nature of caregiving (that it is properly performed by women). Indeed, support for the bill rose significantly after advocates focused on publicizing the act's guarantee of paid time for all working people to care not only for newborns and recently adopted children, but also for a sick spouse or an aging parent.

The expansion of public definitions of care beyond the "woman's domain" of biological reproduction was thus a central message in publicity campaigns after the PFLA became law in April 2016. Throughout the city and its highly trafficked subway and bus system, billboards showcased diverse families and caregiving situations. In one, a white man bent close to a light-skinned woman with black hair whose lips lovingly brushed the dark hair of the baby held to her chest. Above this heterosexual, racially indeterminate family scene, the caption declared, "All parents need time to bond with a new child." In another, a Black man kissed a smiling toddler below the simple statement, "Paid Family Leave is coming to New York," while a third image portrayed a close-up of a wrinkled light-skinned hand being held tenderly between two younger ones. The caption read, "Peace of mind for caregivers . . . You don't have to choose between caring for a loved one and your economic security."

In highlighting these diverse family configurations, the publicity campaigns explicitly worked to de-gender care, a priority reiterated in the numerous in-person and online meetings advocating for temporal labor reform that I attended over the course of my fieldwork. As Ann-Marie Slaughter, a former US State Department director of policy planning, declared in a 2016 webinar on flex-work policies, "Care is not a woman's problem. . . . What we are talking about now is the next half of the movement for full gender equality for women and for men. To finish the business that the second wave of the women's movement began, we have to change male gender roles as much as we've changed female gender roles."[3] In this narrative, policies that enable both women and men to participate equally in productive and reproductive spheres are situated as the next, and possibly final, step in a larger teleology of gendered social progress. This position is not new. Feminists from the nineteenth century onward have imagined a reorganization of gendered labor, pointing out that women's full participation in the labor force is possible only if men become equal partners in domestic and caregiving work. In practice, as we have seen, this ideal remains largely unrealized in the "dualized organization of social reproduction" (Fraser 2016), in

Publicity campaigns for New York's Paid Family Leave Act in a subway car. Photograph by the author.

which middle- and upper-middle-class homes outsource reproductive labor to low-wage women who perform their own care work as unremunerated labor in the home (Boris and Parreñas 2010; Ehrenreich and Hochschild 2003). Regardless of how it is accomplished, time spent in care work continues to be feminized, invisible, and devalued.

The publicity campaigns surrounding the PFLA also sought to re-value reproductive time, reclaiming it from its position subordinate to "productive" working days and centering it within ongoing relations of care. By foregrounding images of loving intergenerational family groups, advocates asserted that care is crucial not only to biological survival but also to the reproduction of authentic and fulfilling human relationships. Yet, at the same time, the chosen images suggest that not all care work carries equal symbolic weight; advocacy materials foregrounded the affective aspects of care rather than the banal, repetitive, and physical labor of toileting, bathing, preparing food, and doing laundry. These tasks remain invisible, reflecting a middle-class cultural context in which the value of care is associated with its affective dimensions, presumed to be freely given, rather than with the low-status and physical domestic labor that is increasingly outsourced to the paid service sector (Nelson 2015).

The political and social context surrounding the act and its eventual passage thus reflected a long-standing tension between the cultural valorization of affective care and a deep ambivalence about material support for care work. In New York State, eligibility requirements for the PFLA are far broader than for the federal FMLA: rather than the twelve months of employment necessary for eligibility under the FMLA, the PFLA states that full-time workers (those who work more than twenty hours per week) must only have worked for twenty-six consecutive weeks for the same employer, while those who work fewer than twenty hours per week must have worked for the same employer for 176 or more nonconsecutive days. Moreover, unlike the FMLA, the PFLA mandates that all private employers, regardless of size, must participate (most state and city employees had already received paid family leave through union contracts prior to the passage of the act).

New York's PFLA is thus an important step in broader claims to temporal justice. Yet issues of class and racial inequality remain embedded in the act, limiting its power to reshape unequal reproductive temporalities. In 2021, the final stage of the law's graduated implementation, paid leave was capped at sixteen weeks at two-thirds of a worker's previous average weekly earnings, provided that this amount did not exceed 67 percent of the average *state* wage (significant for residents of New York City since wages in the more suburban and rural areas of the state are generally lower than in New York City with its high cost of living). For professional women and pregnant people, the use of state-provided paid family leave would likely entail a temporary income decline but, given their generally higher incomes, would be unlikely to have negative long-term effects. However, for low-wage and unstably employed service workers, 67 percent of their previous average weekly earnings might result in less income than the weekly payments of $169 provided by Temporary Disability Insurance (this was particularly true in the law's first stage, when benefits were capped at 50 percent of previous average weekly earnings). Moreover, despite the expansion in eligibility, high variability in working hours and frequent job changes among low-wage service workers may disqualify many from benefits and, until 2022, the law did not apply to domestic workers unless they worked more than forty hours per week for the same employer.[4]

These limitations were not lost on the architects and supporters of the bill. Several people intimately involved in negotiations prior to the bill's passage told me that advocates had engaged in a fierce internal debate about whether to support the current version of the law, which they felt had significant political traction, or to hold out for a more robust version that addressed some of these concerns. An alternative model that had been under serious consideration, for example, had proposed distributing compensation on a sliding scale, rather than as a flat percentage for all income groups, to allow lower-income groups to receive a higher percentage of their previous wages. In the end, advocates agreed to unite behind the current bill, hoping to expand its reach once the idea of paid family leave had become more palatable to the stakeholders who originally opposed it.

Despite the limitations of the PFLA for low-wage workers, the women with whom I discussed the issue universally expressed regret that they would not benefit from the act, at least during their current pregnancy, since it did not go into effect until 2018. Several also articulated the hope that by codifying benefits in law, the PFLA would obviate the need for their frustrating and usually frustrated attempts to negotiate paid leaves with their employers. Their support for the law, as opposed to the ambivalence that many expressed about the effectiveness of the Pregnant Workers Fairness Act, underscores how different interpretive frameworks may shape the reach and power of these policies. While the women I spoke with tended to understand pregnancy-related labor accommodations as reciprocal care for a virtuous worker within "private" interpersonal dynamics, they readily understood state-mandated paid family leave as a universal right of all birthing people to care for their newborns. Through foregrounding the moral imperative of caring for a vulnerable child (as opposed to "simply" care for the pregnant self), they argued for the crucial role of the state in guaranteeing workers time to care.

Conclusion

Movements for temporal justice have the potential to dramatically transform policy, making clear how struggles over care and reproductive time affect not only individual pregnancies but also the well-being of families and households across generational time. Legislation like the Pregnant Workers Fairness Act offers workers an alternative conceptual framework for conceptualizing labor harms, as well as new forms of remediation, providing them with an avenue to challenge injustices through the formal adjudicating bodies of the state (Merry 2009). Yet the persistence of personalism raises the question about the degree to which workers can "code-switch" between the language of rights and idioms of care, with their often conflicting interpretations of harm, justice, and appropriate action, pointing to some of the challenges in implementing policy aimed to improve labor conditions for pregnant workers. By contrast, the women I interviewed saw the PFLA and its efforts to materially and symbolically re-value care work more positively, situating the act within a moral cosmology in which all parents should have the right to time to care for their newborns without economic suffering. Their reactions thus suggest some of the challenges of rights-based efforts to secure temporal and reproductive justice, even as advocates argue that such progressive legislation is vital to a new politics of care.

Epilogue

Time to Care

The experiences of pregnant women as they navigate the temporal regimes of low-wage service work and safety net prenatal care sharply illuminate how intersecting vectors of temporal governance unevenly shape reproductive temporalities, experiences, and outcomes. As people work to reproduce families, communities, and social institutions, their unequal vulnerability to rigid and unforgiving temporal regimes reflects and magnifies durable inequalities across axes of gender, race/ethnicity, class, and immigration status, among others. These personal and collective struggles over time should raise fundamental questions of how we think about and value forms of care in a deeply unequal society.

For the women whose narratives appear in this book, the language of care was a powerful idiom through which they articulated their perception that their persons, time, and pregnancies were valued—or not. In the realms of both work and prenatal care, time was central to their assessments of care or its absence: caring supervisors recognized the competing claims on the time of pregnant service workers and the toll that pregnancy took on their (re)productively laboring bodies. Conversely, those perceived not to care refused to acknowledge women's struggles to navigate conflicts between labor, clinical, and gestational time, denying them needed accommodations to eat, rest, or seek medical care. Similarly, in clinical settings, uncaring health institutions and providers diminished the health and well-being of pregnant patients through forms of temporal governance that deprioritized them and their time, both productive and reproductive. By contrast, caring clinical staff and health institutions respected their patients' time and other commitments, minimizing delays and offering convenient appointment times, and engaged in clinical interactions that made women feel that they, and their pregnancies, mattered.

Care was thus not simply defined instrumentally in the sense of time used "productively" or "wasted." Rather, experiences of care were produced through interactions that were temporal and relational, underscoring the anthropological insight that care is not a time-limited activity but is an ongoing and interactive process through which "people come to matter" (Stevenson 2014). It is generated through practices of recognition, whereby people and institutions acknowledge and carefully attend to someone else's needs over a period of time that may vary from the fleeting duration of a medical appointment or work shift to the span of a lifetime (Buch 2018; Caldwell 2017; García 2010; Muehlebach 2012; Sufrin 2017). In this conceptualization, practices of care bind people together as individuals and as members of groups, producing a sense of value and belonging to a larger social collective (Briggs and Mantini-Briggs 2016; Coe 2019).

Thus, when women condemned individuals or institutions for failing to demonstrate care for them and their needs during pregnancy, they were also describing systems and practices that they felt devalued them, whether in labor or reproduction. Yet, in the clinical setting, often invisible to pregnant patients were the structural conditions that shaped temporal regimes and provider interactions. The ability of providers to give the compassionate and relational care that they might have wanted was deeply compromised by the chronically strained system of safety net care that reflected racialized histories of neglect and disinvestment. From the perspective of providers and staff, their working conditions reflected the state's lack of financial or moral support for the well-being of providers on the frontlines.[1] This too is a form of care (Strong 2020).

Attention to struggles around time as they play out in the reproductive efforts of individuals, kin groups, institutions, and social collectivities thus highlights care as a "concrete work of maintenance with ethical and affective implications and vital politics in interdependent worlds" (Puig de la Bellacasa 2017, 5). In their narratives about time and care, the pregnant women I interviewed tended to focus on the quality of interpersonal relationships, such as those between supervisor and supervised or provider and patient. Yet, as we have seen, such relational and situationally specific conceptions of care can be limiting, encouraging workers to see refusals of accommodation as a lack of care rather than a violation of their rights that could be remediated through appeals to the state. By contrast, advocates for temporal justice argue that attention to time through policy is a crucial and often neglected means to redress inequality (Bear 2016). For them, legislation that protects workers' productive *and* reproductive time from the temporal and material exploitations of capital is an expression of state care and a statement of the equal value of *all* of its citizen-subjects.

The Work of Care under COVID-19

The urgency of these struggles over time and the (gendered) labor of care became starkly apparent when, in March 2020, New York City became the national epicenter of the COVID-19 pandemic. Against the constant wail of ambulance sirens, the city locked down. While those residents with the means fled the city to larger living spaces in less populated suburban and rural areas, those who stayed behind, whether by choice or because of lack of options, faced shuttered schools, long lines at grocery stores, and shortages of everything from toilet paper to Tylenol. COVID-related deaths reached tragic heights that sometimes exceeded eight hundred per day, with thousands more hospitalized. The city's network of public and safety net health institutions, more overburdened and under-resourced than ever, were bursting at the seams, forcing administrators to convert maternity beds to infectious disease wards and erect makeshift tents in any space that they could find. Providers and support staff, working back-to-back shifts for as long as they could physically withstand it, were in constant triage mode, deciding how and where to allot the ever-fewer available beds and ventilators. Everyone was exhausted, traumatized, and afraid.

While most middle-class professionals pivoted quickly to remote work-from-home modalities (leading to new forms of temporal and labor exhaustion like "Zoom fatigue"), those who worked in healthcare, childcare, and critical retail such as grocery stores and pharmacies were designated "essential workers" whose in-person labor was vital to the continued functioning of a pandemic-stricken city. Suddenly, the same people who had long carried out the poorly remunerated and low-status labor of caring for the bodies and the households of others were publicly feted for performing socially necessary, "essential" work. The irony was not lost on anyone, least of all the workers themselves, who continued to perform their jobs for the same or marginally improved pay under conditions of fear, stress, and overwork as co-workers quit, fell sick, or burned out.

The designation of some sectors and occupations as essential brought issues of gender, race, and class into stark relief. Across the country, the pandemic exacerbated conditions of stratified reproduction, highlighting the disconnect between the vocal expressions of public gratitude for the work of essential laborers and the limited social and legal protections for their own and their families' health and well-being. An analysis by the *New York Times* found that one in three jobs held by women was designated essential and that women of color were more likely to be employed in these positions than any other social group, reflecting their disproportionate employment in low-wage service jobs, especially healthcare (Robertson and Gebeloff 2020). Deprioritized for PPE (personal protective equipment) while on the job, these essential workers performed the care and service work that was now understood as socially vital, exposing themselves and their families to COVID-19 as they did so. Mass layoffs in the hotel, restaurant, and retail industries hit low-wage service workers in these sectors in different, albeit no less disruptive ways. One report found that almost 20 percent of Black female workers became unemployed between February and April 2020

(Gould and Wilson 2020), while unknown numbers of undocumented immigrants, often the first to be let go in times of crisis, also lost their jobs. Disproportionately suffering from job loss and reduced hours, one in five Black and Latinx households, and one in three Native American households, reported serious problems affording medical care during the pandemic, increasing the pressure on safety net health institutions and providers who care for underinsured and uninsured people (NPR et al. 2020)

The conditions of pandemic life and labor also exacerbated the gendered, classed, and racial inequalities in reproductive temporalities, since the temporal labor regimes of low-wage workers became even more desynchronized with other reproductive and caregiving commitments. As essential workers left their homes to care for others, they faced their own caregiving dilemmas when daycares and schools closed their doors or pivoted to remote learning. Without the ability of wealthier families to hire private tutors and caregivers, and with their own kin and social networks also likely to be working in essential jobs, some reported having to choose between quitting their jobs and leaving children with little or no supervision while they worked long hours in understaffed facilities. Although some New York City schools later opened to provide desperately needed oversight for the children of essential workers, many families, traumatized by high rates of sickness and death in their communities, decided to keep their children at home to minimize further COVID-19 exposure. As one measure of the crisis facing low-wage workers, in 2021 the Bureau of Labor Statistics reported that the direct care industry, which includes aides in nursing homes, residential homes, and home care, lost 342,000 employees that year alone due to layoffs or resignations (Span 2021).

Stratified Reproduction and Reproductive Health Disparities

The first months of the pandemic were also wracked by another national trauma, as the murder of George Floyd in 2020 lent fuel to anguished protests over police killings and pernicious and persistent racial inequalities. In New York City, the maternal deaths of three young Black women—Cordielle Street, Sha-Asia Washington, and Amber Rose Isaac—between March and July 2020 led to widespread street demonstrations that directly linked racial inequalities to birth injustices. These tragic deaths led also to an impassioned demand for reform from the midwifery service at the safety net hospital where Washington died, as well as demands for more transparency about rates and racial breakdown of maternal deaths, third-trimester fetal losses and stillbirths, and birth-related injuries in various hospitals (Irizarry Aponte 2020). Highlighting Black and brown women's continuing experiences of medical neglect and "diagnostic lapses" (D. Davis 2019), these protests underscored the worsening conditions for prenatal and obstetric care for low-income communities and communities of color during the COVID-19 lockdown (Andaya and Bhatia 2021; Niles et al. 2020). High rates of reproductive morbidity and mortality, activists made clear, are another form of "robbing time" (Coates 2015) from Black pregnant people, their families, and their communities.

For activists, the exacerbation of reproductive health disparities in pandemic conditions thus represented a "crisis within a crisis." Hospitals fearful of transmission barred pregnant people from bringing partners or support persons to prenatal appointments or even, for a short period, to the birthing room, while some also instituted policies of removing healthy newborns from COVID-positive mothers and holding them in the neonatal intensive care unit. As institutions and providers compromised best practices in an effort to minimize transmission of the virus, these distressing birthing conditions were disproportionately likely to be experienced by low-income Black and brown women seeking care at safety net hospitals. Pregnant people with more resources left the city to seek prenatal and obstetric care in places with lower COVID caseloads and fewer birthing restrictions—what one provider at a receiving rural hospital referred to as "COVID refugees." Those with fewer resources had no choice but to rely on safety net hospitals, largely situated in low-income neighborhoods with high numbers of essential workers, that were experiencing surges both in COVID-19 caseloads and in the number of newly uninsured patients, increasing pressure on already stressed providers and institutions. Refrigerated morgue trucks parked outside hospitals (and in at least one case, outside the labor and delivery unit) and medical staff in full protective equipment were constant and visceral reminders to pregnant and birthing people of the threat of sickness and death. Providers, too, were suffering from stress, trauma, and overwork, compromising their own ability to provide quality care. While private health institutions quickly pivoted to telehealth and more welcoming and patient-friendly birthing conditions, safety net hospitals largely lacked both the resources and the technology for these shifts, underscoring the continuing effects of the racialized economization of life in public and safety net healthcare (Andaya and Bhatia 2021).

The worsening of conditions of reproductive care for low-income communities of color in New York City during the pandemic underscores the deeply entrenched nature of these inequities and the extensive work still to be done, despite the state's commitment of funds to task forces and other efforts to ameliorate reproductive health disparities prior to the pandemic. Yet there are some bright spots as well. Recent policies signal a growing recognition of the urgent need for an "infrastructure of care" (Slaughter 2013) to support individual and collective caregiving. In 2018 New York State began its gradual implementation of the provisions guaranteed by the Paid Family Leave Act, which was fully rolled out by 2021. Covering 7.5 million workers in New York State, the program is steadily growing in utilization and in length of leave, with record claims paid out in 2021. Notably, usage is highest among low- and middle-income workers, while men have increased their usage of the program as well (New York State 2022). Eligibility is also expanding; in 2022 domestic workers who worked twenty hours or more (down from forty) for twenty-six weeks or more for the same employer were able to claim paid family leave and, starting in 2023, siblings, including adoptive, half, and step-siblings, also qualified for paid leave to care for each other. In addition, New York State expanded Medicaid coverage in 2021 from the previous sixty days to twelve months after the end of pregnancy, giving otherwise ineligible pregnant people, such as undocumented immigrants, much-needed additional time to seek treatment for birth complications, obtain contraception, or continue care for chronic health conditions. With respect to childcare, after piloting an expansion of the city's free pre-K program to include three-year-old children in 2016, the "3K" program reached capacity in 2020, covering twenty thousand students in fourteen school districts. While not without its problems, this expansion of care has been a boon for low-income parents who previously either depended upon subsidized childcare vouchers that still left childcare expenses out of reach for some, stitched together a patchwork of family care or sometimes substandard informal care, or were forced to withdraw from the workforce. Finally, as New York City emerged from the pandemic, the crucial role played by frontline safety net hospitals and providers in caring for communities most devastated by COVID-19 brought much-needed attention to their plight; in 2022 Governor Kathy Hochul doubled state support for safety net hospitals and petitioned the federal government to increase Medicaid reimbursements in the hope of improving conditions for patients and providers (Goldstein 2022).

More specifically to Beaumont, administrative and leadership changes in the obstetrics and gynecology department have brought renewed attention to the quality of care. Departmental directors and chairs have committed themselves to tackling the stubborn problem of delays and wait times, embarking on the long-term work of improving clinical culture so that both patients and providers feel cared for as they give and receive technical care. While such efforts can be fragile, constrained as they are by bureaucratic inertia, resource scarcity, and the whims of higher-ups, they are a reminder that other ways of institutional care are possible.

A (Slowly) Changing Landscape of Labor and Policy

In small ways and large, in policy and practice, struggles over time and care are at the forefront of contemporary movements for change. Since the conclusion of my ethnographic fieldwork in 2016, low-wage workers and their allies in New York City have successfully fought for legislation that publicly recognizes the value of their time, from hourly pay to schedule stability. One victory was the increase in the minimum wage, beginning on December 31, 2019, to fifteen dollars per hour, the result of a long-fought battle by workers and their advocates, known as #FightforFifteen, that began in 2012 when two hundred fast-food workers in New York City walked off the job to protest low wages, poor working conditions, and union-blocking by management. Growing rapidly to become a national movement, #FightforFifteen has tallied some vital successes in cities across the United States, as well as among federal employees, although as of the beginning of 2023 only three states had reached a minimum wage of fifteen dollars per hour or over.[2] In New York City the success of #FightforFifteen spurred legislation that increased the minimum wage of home health aides to seventeen dollars per hour in 2022. While still barely above the new minimum wage floor and insufficient for the increased cost of post-pandemic living, this represents a significant bump from the ten dollars per hour that most of the aides whom I interviewed reported earning during my fieldwork.

Other laws have specifically sought to use state power to rein in exploitative forms of corporate temporal governance. In 2017 New York City's Fair Workweek Law went into effect, mandating that employers in fast-food and retail compensate workers if shifts are canceled with fewer than seventy-two hours' notice and that they pay a premium for shifts added in this same timeframe. The law also bans the widely reviled "clopenings" and encourages employers to commit to providing workers with stable schedules at least two weeks in advance. Expanding these efforts to protect workers' time, in November 2022 New York State governor Kathy Hochul signed new legislation aimed at curtailing abusive work attendance policies, such as employers' use of demerits for lawfully protected absences like attending urgent medical appointments. For pregnant workers like Sabrina Georges, who was punished with a demerit when she sought medical care for her preterm contractions, this is welcome news indeed. Finally, as of the time of writing, members of the New York City Council were considering a new bill, "No More 24," which would ban the industry-wide practice of assigning home health aides to a twenty-four-hour shift while paying them only for thirteen hours of work. Home health aides speaking in support of the bill made clear the bad faith embedded in the assumption that the eleven unpaid hours were for the aide's leisure and sleep: Li Qin, who worked three consecutive twenty-four-hour shifts per week for three years, told reporters, "In the day I had to look after my patients [a couple] the whole time to prevent them from falling down . . . and at night I had to turn the bodies of the patients every two hours and change their diapers and carry them to the bathroom. It's impossible for me to have five hours of sleep" (Khafagy 2022).

Across the nation, activists in a growing number of cities and states have engaged in social media and lobbying campaigns, such as #OurTimeCounts, that draw attention to workers whose lives are destabilized by constantly changing and unpredictable work schedules. Linking the protection of workers' productive and reproductive time to assertions of care and shared humanity, a 2019 petition in Washington State challenged the normalization of abusive scheduling practices, stating, "Workers are humans too—we need time to spend with our families, take classes, work a second job, or just take care of ourselves." But it is not only low-wage service workers whose calls for temporal justice rest on an affirmation that they are humans rather than well-regulated machines. As this book went to press, medical residents at the University of Pennsylvania were seeking to unionize for better pay, hours, and benefits, including family leave. In an echo of the language used in Washington State, a spokesperson for the medical residents told the press, "We

An electronic advertisement on the side of a New York City trash can promotes the city's Fair Workweek Law. Photograph by the author.

are human beings first and foremost. If we're sacrificing our physical and mental health, our financial stability, and our personal relationships in order to provide care, that means that our healthcare system is failing" (Mancini 2023). Tying together time and social justice, such movements argue that caring states must defend workers' ability to predict and plan their time in meaningful ways, to take time to care for themselves and their loved ones, and to otherwise resist encroachment by institutions and individuals that see their time as available and disposable (Goodin et al. 2008).

There have also been important legislative victories for pregnant, postpartum, and nursing workers. Between 2014—when New York City became the first locality to pass a Pregnant Workers Fairness Act—and 2022, thirty states and the District of Columbia passed versions of this act. On December 29, 2022, after a decade of lobbying efforts, a federal Pregnant Workers Fairness Act and the PUMP for Nursing Mothers (which mandates that nursing workers be provided with a private space and break time to pump breast milk) was finally signed into law as part of an omnibus bill. Backed by robust enforcement provisions, these laws require employers to provide reasonable accommodations to pregnant, postpartum, and nursing workers without penalty, extending new and meaningful rights to millions of workers across the nation.[3]

Yet in other areas, policy change has been slow. Despite ongoing lobbying efforts, as of 2023 only eleven states had enacted paid family leave legislation. Moreover, there is still no movement on federal bills to protect workers from exploitative scheduling practices or to protect the rights of part-time workers, while efforts to raise the federal minimum wage, most recently in the 2021 American Rescue Plan Act, have stalled in the Senate. At the national level, it has been the exigencies of the market rather than federal policy that has boosted the bargaining power of low-wage workers, although these benefits may prove to be temporary. As the world inched out of lockdown beginning in early 2021, demand for consumer goods and service surged, and businesses sought to take on employees only to find that the labor market was the tightest it had been in decades (Goldberg 2021; Irwin 2021). With employers desperate to attract and retain workers, low-wage service employees have been newly empowered to demand better working conditions and higher pay (Lohr 2021; Porter 2021). Yet even in an economy in which workers purportedly enjoy increased bargaining power, researchers have found little change in scheduling practices in low-wage service work, particularly with respect to part-time and unpredictable work schedules (Scheiber 2022). A twice-yearly national survey found that a quarter of respondents in retail and food service were scheduled for fewer than thirty-five hours a week, despite a preference for more hours. Workers of color, and women of color in particular, continued to be disproportionately vulnerable to insufficient and unpredictable schedules (Zundl et al. 2022).

Such findings underscore that not all workers are equally positioned in a booming labor market. Low-income working people with caregiving responsibilities are at a particular disadvantage, since the institutions of childcare and eldercare upon which many depend to work outside the home have not fully recuperated from the pandemic. As of 2022, one in ten childcare providers had not returned to work and staffing in nursing homes was 11 percent lower than in February 2020 (DePillis, Smialek, and Casselman 2022). Given this crumbling infrastructure of care, some low-wage service workers have little choice but to remain out of the paid workforce, leading to further workforce shortages. As Katherine Gallagher Robbins, a senior fellow with the National Partnership for Women and Families, stated, "For women, that's the double whammy—most of those workers are women, and most of the people who need those supports to enter the work force themselves are women" (DePillis, Smialek, and Casselman 2022).

The ongoing crisis of care that constrains women's ability to enter a flourishing labor market is even more troubling given skyrocketing inflation rates, a consequence of various global crises from COVID-related breakdowns in supply chains to climate change–related disruptions and Russia's invasion of Ukraine. Reports have found that despite rising wages, low-income families are actually spending a greater share of their income on basic necessities than they had prior to the pandemic (Dickler 2022). As always, falling real wages (the actual purchasing power of workers' income) impact low-income families first and hardest, increasing their vulnerability and forcing them to look for additional sources of earnings or support. In conditions of scarcity, other forms of invisible labor proliferate as people in low-resource families, particularly women, spend more of their precious leisure time in seeking out grocery and retail bargains, recalibrating household budgets, and otherwise reassessing individual and familial priorities. The very real consequences for low-wage workers and their families underscore the limits of the market in protecting vulnerable groups, calling attention to the urgent need for policy protections at the local, state, and federal levels.

Toward a Conclusion

In his account of the transformation of the Pittsburgh economy from steelworking to healthcare, Gabriel Winant reminds us that "collective life [is] always constituted out of a time discipline and the struggles it engender[s]" (2021, 74). Individual and social lives are produced, woven together, and (re)configured through relationships that are profoundly, and unequally, shaped by temporal regimes. The governance of time and the conditions of life that it engenders are thus powerful means through which hierarchies and inequalities of race/ethnicity, gender, disability, sexuality, class, and documentation status, among others, are brought into being in social life—experienced, concretized, and reproduced in the temporalities of individual and collective bodies. As scholar-activists writing from the perspective of disability, labor, gender, and racial justice make abundantly clear, the inequities built into social constructions of "normative time" harm us all (B. Cooper 2017; Hendren 2020).

The relationship between temporal and reproductive governance has also recently emerged as an urgent political issue, albeit for different reasons that those that this book addresses, with the 2022 Supreme Court decision that rolled back constitutional rights to abortion care. Even prior to the *Dobbs* ruling, low-income pregnant people living in states with restrictive abortion laws often struggled to access abortion care across county or state borders, which meant incurring costs for transportation, hotel rooms, and childcare, in addition to the loss of income due to missed work. The virtual elimination of abortion care in many states now forces pregnant people to travel longer distances for care; with increased distances, expenses and obstacles become more complex and more difficult to navigate. While they wait to accumulate funds or to work out the necessary logistics, some may end up with later-stage abortions that carry higher maternal risk. Others will hit the gestational age limits for legal abortion in the states that they can most readily access, forcing them to continue with an undesired pregnancy. Restrictive abortion laws, like other punitive forms of temporal and reproductive governance, thus fall heaviest on low-resource individuals and communities, disproportionately those of color, underscoring the urgency of struggles for reproductive justice and its affirmation of the right of all people to choose the number and timing of their pregnancies, and to raise their children in safe and dignified conditions (Ross and Solinger 2017).

Whether it takes place in households, workplaces, hospitals, or public forums, efforts to undo injurious forms of temporal governance underscore the sustained and collective political labor required to envision and construct social and cultural futures shaped by justice and compassion. This means engaging, as María Puig de la Bellacasa puts it, in a "thick impure involvement in a world where the question of how to care needs to be posed" (2017, 6). As we work to reproduce and nurture children, families, and meaningful social collectives of all kinds, the fight for temporal justice is one step toward imagining a different world for us all, one that recognizes the time that we all need to care.

ACKNOWLEDGMENTS

There are so many people who make it possible for a project like this to come to fruition; I am humbled and filled with gratitude when I think about all of the debts that I have accumulated over the years of research and writing. Memory is always partial, and if I have failed to recollect the whole in this brief summary, know that your contributions were seen and appreciated. All other errors and omissions in the book, of course, are also my own.

    I am profoundly grateful to all the participants in this research, who were willing to trust a stranger with their time and their insights. I hope that this book does justice to your experiences and lends strength to your calls for temporal structures that allow people to care for themselves and for others. Beyond them, I owe the most to the ob-gyn whom I call Dr. Silva, who facilitated my access to Beaumont Hospital, smoothed my entrance into the field through introductions to everyone from high-level administrators to reception staff, and was a gracious and generous interlocutor both during and after my fieldwork. I feel beyond fortunate that our children brought our families into each other's orbits when they did—our lives are more filled with the many riches of friendship because of them. I am also deeply thankful to "Dr. Becker," the administrator who green-lighted my presence in the obstetrics department, to Dr. Laura Benson, a resident at Beaumont during the time that I spent there, for research assistance and her rich ethnographic insights, as well as to all the clinical and reception staff who welcomed me and tolerated my questions despite the many other claims to their time. My gratitude also goes out to Christina Pili, who in 2015 was the director of research administration in the Office of Health Improvement at New York City Health and Hospitals. Although she may not remember, her willingness to go above and beyond to resolve the financial and logistical problems that arose once we discovered that Beaumont did not have a standing IRB to review this research allowed this project to go forward when I thought—for the umpteenth time—that it might not.

The seeds of this project were sown when Dr. Annis Golden and Dr. Caryn Medved invited me to join them as a researcher in a qualitative study on the conflicts between work and healthcare scheduling among low-income residents of a small city in New York's Hudson Valley. Our lively discussions about the interview findings were generative, leading me to wonder how time and work scheduling might shape experiences of pregnancy and prenatal care, areas that I had previously investigated in the Cuban context. When I was still feeling my way through a new field of literature and policy, Dr. Mimi Niles helped me think through the politics of work in public prenatal care. Harry Belafonte introduced me to the service union SEIU 1199, where I learned about union organizing for home health care workers. Dan Gross, then the executive director of the workers' organizing initiative Brandworkers, led me to Sarah Madden, whose thoughtful analysis and "double consciousness" as a barista and union organizer helped me to understand the questions that I needed to ask. In the early days of research, Dr. Wendy Chavkin extended a generous invitation to join Columbia University's "Work/Family in the 21st Century" working group, where I had the great good fortune to sit in a room with many luminaries of work-life research. Although no doubt many were perplexed by my presence, the opportunity to participate in discussions and listen to research presentations and policy briefs on work-life policy greatly enriched my understanding of the research-policy nexus in this area.

Writing is a solitary activity, and I thank the organizers of several workshops and speaking engagements for the opportunity to share my work and hone my analysis in the company of colleagues who are both generous and rigorous in their thinking. On the lovely campus of the School for Advanced Research at Santa Fe, delicious food and conversations with Jessica Mulligan, Heide Castañeda, Cathleen Willging, Emily

Brunson, Tiffany Joseph, Mary Alice Scott, Susan Sered, and Susan Shaw nourished the body and mind. A Wenner-Gren workshop in New York City, organized by Daisy Deomampo and Natalí Váldez, provided a collegial and intellectually stimulating environment to workshop material alongside Dána-Ain Davis, Alyshia Gálvez, Jeanne Flavin, Risa Cromer, Nessette Falu, Tessa Moll, Lynn Roberts, Abril Saldana, and Sandra Bärnreuther. A 2016 American Anthropological Association panel on gender and time, which resulted in a co-edited issue of *Voices*, as well as the opportunity to present material to members of the New York State Department of Health through the University at Albany's Maternal and Child Health Program brown bag series, also contributed to the analysis. I am grateful to Rachel Fleming, Christine Bozlak, and Rachel de Long for their interest and support.

The University at Albany supported this research through a Faculty Research Grant. I also thank my colleagues in the anthropology department who provided a supportive environment for academic life over the long years that this project took shape: Jennifer Burrell, Louise Burkhart, Walter Little, Jim Collins, Marilyn Masson, Rob Rosenswig, Sean Rafferty, Chris Wolff, Lee Bickmore, Lauren Clemens, John Justeson, Adam Gordon, John Polk, John Rowan, Amanda Spriggs, and Veronica Pérez Rodriguez, as well as to Rajani Bhatia and Barbara Sutton in Women's, Gender, and Sexuality Studies. Our conversations on everything from research to family to the joys and tribulations of teaching have enriched my thinking and helped me to maintain a healthy perspective on my own work-life balance.

There are so many other treasured friends and colleagues whose support has meant the world to me over the years. Eleana Kim, Julie Chu, Amy Cooper, Simon May, Melanie Madeiros, Jennifer Guzmán, Sherine Hamdy, Jessica Cattelino, and Amahl Bishara, among others, have made academia a more welcoming place. Friendships with the John Street Collective—Jennifer Ellice, Jenny Strodl, Jennie Urman, Victoria Webster, and Sabrina Dupré—have nurtured me, from close and afar, for almost thirty years. In Brooklyn, Andrew and Juliette Michaelson, Tanya and Jack Ohly, Elissa and Zach Gelber, Rachel Lotus, Davina Pardo, Andrew Blum, Nell Hirschman-Levy, Bridgette Bissonette, Manu Goswami, Greg Grandin, Karl and Joan Nelson, Kat Aaron, Josh Breitbart, and Marlene and Jay Wallace offered companionship and encouragement, arranged playdates when I needed work coverage and after-school pickups, and in every way just made parenting more fun. Billiam van Roestenberg gave us a place to stay in New Paltz during the frightening first months that the pandemic devastated New York City. Once we returned, parents from the Pangolins learning pod—Ellen McCrum, Matt Leiber, Melih and Micky Onvural, Itai and Anne-Elizabeth Kaitano, Kirk Seward, and Audrey Cooper—and its wonderful and intrepid teacher, Dora Finkelstein, sustained my whole family through a year of remote learning and brought laughter and togetherness to a dark time. I cherish you all.

At New York University Press, my editor, Jennifer Hammer, reached out to me about this project when it was the barest sketch of an idea and helped me see what was interesting about it. Her support over the years and efficient shepherding through the editorial process brought this book into being far earlier than might otherwise have been the case. I thank Veronica Knutson and the editorial, marketing, and production team for all their work. As is always the case in academia, this work has relied on the intellectual labor of anonymous others who have constantly held me to a higher standard. I am deeply grateful to the two reviewers who provided detailed and generous feedback on several versions of this manuscript that immeasurably improved the final product. Anonymous reviewers for the journal *Medical Anthropology* and its editor, Lenore Manderson, strengthened an article based on chapter 3, and many of their suggestions were incorporated into this final manuscript.

Over the years that I thought and wrote about work, reproduction, and time, the love and encouragement of my own dear family surrounded me when the grueling labor of writing felt overwhelming, and provided childcare, meals, support, sounding boards, and much-needed diversion at crucial moments. Pamela and Harry Belafonte, Peter Frank,

Randy Bloom, Sarah Frank, Bill Scanga, and Olive Scanga—I couldn't have asked to have married into a better family. Harry, your untiring work for social justice changed the world. Your fierce spirit and generous soul will be forever missed.

In Hawai'i, my mother, Barbara Watson Andaya, has brought her attention to detail, thoughtful questions, and curiosity to my own work from my earliest childhood. Mum, I am a better academic because of you. I also thank my father, Leonard Andaya, and sister and brother-in-law, Alexis and Masa Hamasaki, and their children, Caleb, Bryce, Drew, and Abby, for all of the love and soul-nourishing laughter. Of my husband, Lindsey Frank, and children, Mateo and Zoe, words fail me. I am grateful that you are here with me, and for the intertwining of our lives. The joy and adventure that you bring to moments small and large remind me of what is meaningful and worthwhile in the world, and of the preciousness of our time together.

NOTES

INTRODUCTION

1. All names of individuals and institutions are pseudonyms.
2. The Paid Sick Leave Law was later amended to include a broader definition of family members as well as time to seek care for victims of intimate partner violence. Renamed the Paid Safe and Sick Leave Act, these amendments took effect in 2018. For consistency with the present, I use the act's current name throughout the book.
3. In an earlier publication (Andaya 2017), I had referred to this concept as *clinical temporalities*. In this book, I use *clinical time* to bring it into alignment with *labor time* and *gestational time*.
4. In her analysis of unhoused women who use substances while pregnant, anthropologist Kelly Ray Knight uses the term "pregnancy time" to name one form of temporality that constrains women's options. While informed by this analysis, I prefer "gestational time" for its sense of the *duration* of pregnancy (especially in the trimesters measured by clinicians), as well as the temporal and cyclical rhythms of gestation itself.
5. Data drawn from reports published by Beaumont Hospital. To maintain confidentiality, I do not cite internal reports that name the hospital.
6. The Special Supplemental Nutrition Program for Women, Infants and Children (WIC) is a federal assistance program for eligible low-income pregnant, breastfeeding, and non-breastfeeding postpartum women, infants, and children up to five years who are at nutritional risk.
7. The Supplemental Nutrition Assistance Program, popularly known as "food stamps."
8. The single person not enrolled in Medicaid was an immigrant who chose to pay out of pocket, fearful that usage of the Medicaid program would count against her in her efforts to secure citizenship.

CHAPTER 3. CLINICAL TIME AND RACIALIZED INEQUALITY IN SAFETY NET PRENATAL CARE

1. The term "redlining" refers to racial discrimination in housing, particularly through practices of denying government-backed mortgages or home insurance in areas considered "risky investments" (which were marked as red zones in government maps beginning in the New Deal of the 1930s). Unsurprisingly, these

zones were neighborhoods where Black families and families of color tended to live, who were thus largely blocked from purchasing homes through their inability to access the lower-interest and more secure mortgages offered by the government.

2 Many insurers reimburse safety net hospitals at lower rates than they reimburse private hospitals, even for the same procedure. Moreover, even measures intended to improve health have been deeply impacted by US politics. The 2010 Affordable Care Act mandated that states increase income thresholds for Medicaid eligibility and that all individuals not covered by either public or employer-based insurance purchase a health insurance plan (the "individual mandate"). The act also reduced Medicaid reimbursement rates in the expectation that hospitals would be less burdened by the cost of treating uninsured individuals, and that insurance payouts from the greater number of publicly and privately insured patients would make up any income difference. A 2012 Supreme Court decision overturning the individual mandate, as well as the decision by some Republican states not to expand Medicaid eligibility, left the act in disarray. Although New York State did expand Medicaid eligibility, the reductions in Medicaid reimbursements have proved disastrous for New York City's safety net hospitals, since many of their patients are undocumented immigrants who remained ineligible for Medicaid coverage under the Affordable Care Act.

CHAPTER 4. COSMOLOGIES OF CARE

1 See "What Are Human Rights?," United Nations, Office of the High Commissioner on Human Rights, www.ohchr.org.
2 See "Inside the NYC Commission on Human Rights," www1.nyc.gov.
3 "A Conversation with Anne-Marie Slaughter on Women, Men, Work, and Family," Third Path Institute, June 9, 2016, https://thirdpath.org.
4 As of January 1, 2022, eligibility for domestic workers was changed to allow those who worked for the same private employer for twenty hours or more for twenty-six consecutive weeks or more.

EPILOGUE

1 As this book went to press, New York City was facing a threatened strike by nurses employed in its public hospitals, who were protesting the "dangerous conditions" produced by chronic understaffing and, consequently, extremely high nurse-patient ratios. This understaffing, they pointed out, led to poorer quality of patient care and high levels of stress and burnout for nurses.
2 These are Washington, California, and Massachusetts.
3 In some states, like New York, the state version of the Pregnant Workers Fairness Act offers more extensive protections than the federal one, and remains in place. In states with more limited or no such act, the passage of this legislation is an important victory.

BIBLIOGRAPHY

Alber, Erdmute, and Heike Drotbohm. 2015. *Anthropological Perspectives on Care: Work, Kinship, and the Life-Course.* New York: Palgrave Macmillan.

Andaya, Elise. 2014. *Conceiving Cuba: Reproduction, Women, and the State in the Post-Soviet Era.* New Brunswick: Rutgers University Press.

———. 2017. "Stratification through Medicaid: Public Prenatal Care in New York City." In *Unequal Coverage: The Experience of Health Care Reform in the United States,* edited by Jessica M. Mulligan and Heide Castañeda, 102–26. New York: New York University Press.

Andaya, Elise, and Rajani Bhatia. 2021. *The Impact of COVID-19 on Minority Disparities in Sexual and Reproductive Health Care in New York State.* Albany: University at Albany.

Appelbaum, Binyamin. 2016. "The Millions of Americans Donald Trump and Hillary Clinton Barely Mention: The Poor." *New York Times,* August 11.

Auyero, Javier. 2012. *Patients of the State: The Politics of Waiting in Argentina.* Durham: Duke University Press.

Badger, Emily, Claire Cain Miller, Adam Pearce, and Kevin Quealy. 2018. "Extensive Data Shows Punishing Reach of Racism for Black Boys." *New York Times,* March 19.

Badger, Emily, Margot Sanger-Katz, Claire Cain Miller, and Eve Washington. 2022. "Ragged Safety Net Is Weaker in States That Ban Abortion." *New York Times,* July 30.

Bakhtin, Mikhail Mikhaïlovich. 2010. *The Dialogic Imagination: Four Essays.* Austin: University of Texas Press.

Bakst, Dina, Elizabeth Gedmark, and Sarah Brafman. 2019. *Long Overdue: It Is Time for the Federal Pregnant Workers Fairness Act.* New York: A Better Balance.

Barnes, Mitchell, Lauren Bauer, and Wendy Edelberg. 2022. *Nine Facts about the Service Sector in the United States.* Washington, DC: Brookings Institution.

Barnes, Riché J. Daniel. 2015. *Raising the Race: Black Career Women Redefine Marriage, Motherhood, and Community.* New Brunswick: Rutgers University Press.

Barrón-López, Laura, and Dana Liebelson. 2015. "Paul Ryan Gives His Staff Paid Family Leave. No, He Doesn't Want It Guaranteed for You." *Huffington Post,* October 23.

Bear, Laura. 2016. "Time as Technique." *Annual Review of Anthropology* 45:487–502.

Berlant, Lauren. 2011. "A Properly Political Concept of Love: Three Approaches in Ten Pages." *Cultural Anthropology* 24(4): 683–91.

A Better Balance. 2020. *Misled & Misinformed: How Some US Employers Use "No Fault" Attendance Policies to Trample on Workers' Rights.* New York: A Better Balance.

———. 2021a. An Unprecedented Crisis of Care: Building Better Workplace Policies for Working Families. Webinar.

———. 2021b. The Crisis of Care: Work, Family, and Caregiving in COVID-Era New York. Webinar. A Better Balance and the Office of the Comptroller, Scott Stringer.

———. 2022. "29 Years of the FMLA: The New Paid Leave Frontier Ahead." February 3. www.abetterbalance.org. Accessed February 23, 2022.

Bharadwaj, Aditya. 2016. *Conceptions: Infertility and Procreative Technologies in India*. New York: Berghahn.

Biehl, João. 2012. "Care and Disregard." In *A Companion to Moral Anthropology*, edited by Didier Fassin, 242–63. Malden, MA: Wiley Blackwell.

Bjork, Collin, and Frida Buhre. 2021. "Resisting Temporal Regimes, Imagining Just Temporalities." *Rhetoric Society Quarterly* 51(3): 177–81.

Bonde, Jens Peter E., Kristian Tore Jørgensen, Matteo Bonzini, and Keith T. Palmer. 2013. "Risk of Miscarriage and Occupational Activity: A Systematic Review and Meta-Analysis Regarding Shift Work, Working Hours, Lifting, Standing and Physical Workload." *Scandinavian Journal of Work, Environment & Health* 39(4): 325–34.

Bordo, Susan. 1997. "The Body and the Reproduction of Femininity." In *Writing on the Body: Female Embodiment and Feminist Theory*, edited by Katie Conboy and Nadia Medina, 90–113. New York: Columbia University Press.

Boris, Eileen, and Rhacel Salazar Parreñas, eds. 2010. *Intimate Labors: Cultures, Technologies, and the Politics of Care*. Palo Alto, CA: Stanford University Press.

Bourgois, Philippe. 1988. "Conjugated Oppression: Class and Ethnicity among Guaymi and Kuna Banana Workers." *American Ethnologist* 15(2): 328–48.

———. 2003. *In Search of Respect: Selling Crack in El Barrio*. Cambridge, UK: Cambridge University Press.

Boushey, Heather. 2016. *Finding Time: The Economics of Work-Life Conflict*. Cambridge, MA: Harvard University Press.

Boushey, Heather, and Sarah Jane Glynn. 2012. *There Are Significant Business Costs to Replacing Employees*. Washington, DC: Center for American Progress.

Bridges, Khiara. 2011. *Reproducing Race: An Ethnography of Pregnancy as a Site of Racialization*. Berkeley: University of California Press.

———. 2017. *The Poverty of Privacy Rights*. Palo Alto, CA: Stanford University Press.

Briggs, Charles L., and Clara Mantini-Briggs. 2016. *Tell Me Why My Children Died: Rabies, Indigenous Knowledge, and Communicative Justice*. Durham: Duke University Press.

Briggs, Laura. 2017. *How All Politics Became Reproductive Politics: From Welfare Reform to Foreclosure to Trump*. Berkeley: University of California Press.

Brodkin Sacks, Karen. 1998. *How Jews Became White Folks and What That Says about Race in America*. New Brunswick: Rutgers University Press.

Brodwin, Paul. 2013. *Everyday Ethics: Voices from the Frontline of Community Psychiatry*. Berkeley: University of California Press.

Buch, Elana D. 2018. *Inequalities of Aging: Paradoxes of Independence in American Home Care*. New York: New York University Press.
Burrell, Jennifer. 2010. "In and Out of Rights: Security, Migration, and Human Rights Talk in Postwar Guatemala." *Journal of Latin American and Caribbean Anthropology* 15(1): 90–115.
Business Insider. 2019. *The US Home Healthcare Report*. New York: Business Insider.
Butler, Judith. 2004. *Precarious Life: The Powers of Mourning and Violence*. New York: Verso.
———. 2009. "Performativity, Precarity, and Sexual Politics." *Revista de Antropología Iberoamericana* 4(3): i–xiii.
Cai, Chenxi, Ben Vandermeer, Rshmi Khurana, Kara Nerenberg, Robin Featherstone, Meghan Sebastianski, and Margie H. Davenport. 2019. "The Impact of Occupational Shift Work and Working Hours during Pregnancy on Health Outcomes: A Systematic Review and Meta-Analysis." *American Journal of Obstetrics and Gynecology* 221(6): 563–76.
Caldwell, Melissa. 2017. *Living Faithfully in an Unjust World: Compassionate Care in Russia*. Berkeley: University of California Press.
Carp, Alex. 2022. "Steven Banks vs. Homelessness." *New York Times Magazine*, February 6.
Carrillo, Dani, Kristen Harknett, Allison Logan, Sigrid Luhr, and Daniel Schneider. 2017. "Instability of Work and Care: How Work Schedules Shape Child-Care Arrangements for Parents Working in the Service Sector." *Social Service Review* 91(3): 422–55.
CFI. 2021. "Service Sector." www.corporatefinance.institute. Accessed September 9, 2021.
Chary, Anita, David Flood, Kirsten Austad, Jillian Moore, Nora King, Boris Martinez, Pablo Garcia, Waleska Lopez, Shom Dasgupta-Tsikinas, and Peter Rohloff. 2016. "Navigating Bureaucracy: Accompanying Indigenous Maya Patients with Complex Health Care Needs in Guatemala." *Human Organization* 75(4): 305–14.
Chokshi, Dave A., Ji E. Chang, and Ross M. Wilson. 2016. "Health Reform and the Changing Safety Net in the United States." *New England Journal of Medicine* 375(18): 1790–96. https://doi.org/10.1056/NEJMhpr1608578.
Clawson, Dan, and Naomi Gerstel. 2014. *Unequal Time: Gender, Class, and Family in Employment Schedules*. New York: Russell Sage Foundation.
Coates, Ta-Nehisi. 2015. *Between the World and Me*. New York: Spiegel and Grau.
Coe, Cati. 2019. *The New American Servitude: Political Belonging among African Immigrant Home Care Workers*. New York: New York University Press.
Colen, Shellee. 1995. "'Like a Mother to Them': Stratified Reproduction and West Indian Childcare Workers and Employers in New York." In *Conceiving the New World Order: The Global Politics of Reproduction*, edited by Faye Ginsburg and Rayna Rapp, 78–102. Berkeley: University of California Press.
Cooper, Amy. 2015. "Time Seizures and the Self: Institutional Temporalities and Self Preservation among Homeless Women." *Culture, Medicine and Psychiatry* 39(1): 162–85.

Cooper, Brittney. 2017. "The Racial Politics of Time." TED talk, February 21.
Cooper, Frederick, and Ann Laura Stoler. 1997. *Tensions of Empire: Colonial Cultures in a Bourgeois World*. Berkeley: University of California Press.
Cooper, Melinda, and Catherine Waldby. 2014. *Clinical Labor: Tissue Donors and Research Subjects in the Global Bioeconomy*. Durham: Duke University Press.
Daniels, Pamela, Godfrey Fuji Noe, and Robert Mayberry. 2006. "Barriers to Prenatal Care among Black Women of Low Socioeconomic Status." *American Journal of Health Behavior* 30(2): 188–98.
Davis, Angela Y. 1981. *Women, Race, and Class*. New York: Random House.
Davis, Dána-Ain. 2019. *Reproductive Injustice: Racism, Pregnancy, and Premature Birth*. New York: New York University Press.
Davis-Floyd, Robbie E. 2004. *Birth as an American Rite of Passage*. Berkeley: University of California Press.
Dell'Antonia, K. J. 2016. "For US Parents, a Troubling Happiness Gap." *New York Times*, June 17. https://well.blogs.nytimes.com.
Deomampo, Daisy. 2016. *Transnational Reproduction: Race, Kinship, and Commercial Surrogacy in India*. New York: New York University Press.
DePillis, Lydia, Jeanna Smialek, and Ben Casselman. 2022. "Jobs Aplenty, but a Shortage of Care Keeps Many Women from Benefiting." *New York Times*, July 7.
Desmond, Matthew. 2016. *Evicted: Poverty and Profit in the American City*. New York: Broadway Books.
———. 2023. "A Problem We Can't Seem to Fix: Why Is Poverty in America So Intractable?" *New York Times Magazine*, March 12.
DeVoe, Sanford E., and Jeffrey Pfeffer. 2007. "When Time Is Money: The Effect of Hourly Payment on the Evaluation of Time." *Organizational Behavior and Human Decision Processes* 104(1): 1–13.
Dickler, Jessica. 2022. "Amid Rising Prices, American Families Fall Deeper in Debt." CNBC, January 11. CNBC.com.
Edin, Kathryn, and Laura Lein. 1997. *Making Ends Meet: How Single Mothers Survive Welfare and Low-Wage Work*. New York: Russell Sage Foundation.
Ehrenreich, Barbara, and Arlie Russell Hochschild. 2003. *Global Woman: Nannies, Maids, and Sex Workers in the New Economy*. New York: Macmillan.
Fabian, Johannes. 1983. *Time and the Other: How Anthropology Makes Its Object*. New York: Columbia University Press.
Foucault, Michel. 1982. "The Subject and Power." *Critical Inquiry* 8(4): 777–95.
Francis, Ellen, Helier Cheung, and Miriam Berger. 2021. "How Does the US Compare to Other Countries on Paid Parental Leave? Americans Get 0 Weeks. Estonians Get More Than 80." *Washington Post*, November 11.
Fraser, Nancy. 2016. "Contradictions of Capital and Care." *New Left Review* 100(99): 99–117.
Gálvez, Alyshia. 2011. *Patient Citizens, Immigrant Mothers: Mexican Women, Public Prenatal Care, and the Birth Weight Paradox*. New Brunswick: Rutgers University Press.

García, Angela. 2010. *The Pastoral Clinic: Addiction and Dispossession along the Rio Grande*. Berkeley: University of California Press.

Gay, Mara. 2017. "Thousands of Working New Yorkers Are Living in Homeless Shelters." *Wall Street Journal*, April 10.

GBD 2015 Maternal Mortality Collaborators. 2016. "Global, Regional, and National Levels of Maternal Mortality, 1990–2015: A Systematic Analysis for the Global Burden of Disease Study 2015." *Lancet* 388:1775–1812.

Gemmill, Alison, Ralph Catalano, Joan A. Casey, Deborah Karasek, Héctor E. Alcalá, Holly Elser, and Jacqueline M. Torres. 2019. "Association of Preterm Births among US Latina Women with the 2016 Presidential Election." *Journal of the American Medical Association* 2(7): e197084.

Georges, Eugenia. 2008. *Bodies of Knowledge: The Medicalization of Reproduction in Greece*. Nashville: Vanderbilt University Press.

Geronimus, Arline T. 1992. "The Weathering Hypothesis and the Health of African-American Women and Infants: Evidence and Speculations." *Ethnicity & Disease* 2(3): 207–21.

Ginsburg, Faye, and Rayna Rapp, eds. 1995. *Conceiving the New World Order: The Global Politics of Reproduction*. Berkeley: University of California Press.

Gitis, Ben, Emerson Sprick, and Adrienne Schweer. 2022. *Morning Consult: 1 in 5 Moms Experience Pregnancy Discrimination in the Workplace*. Washington, DC: Bipartisan Policy Center.

Glaser, Alana Lee. 2020. "Collective Complaint: Immigrant Women Caregivers' Community, Performance, and the Limits of Labor Law in New York City." *PoLAR: Political and Legal Anthropology Review* 43(2): 195–210.

Glenn, Evelyn Nakano. 1992. "From Servitude to Service Work: Historical Continuities in the Racial Division of Paid Reproductive Labor." *Signs: Journal of Women in Culture and Society* 18(1): 1–43.

Goffman, Erving. (1963) 1986. *Stigma: Notes on a Spoiled Identity*. New York: Touchstone Press.

Goldberg, Emma. 2021. "In a 'Workers Economy,' Who Really Holds the Cards?" *New York Times*, November 21.

Golden, Annis, Caryn Medved, and Elise Andaya. 2023. "I Never Even Tried to Get out of Work: Low Wage Service Work, Work-Life Interrelationships, and Women's Health in the United States." *Journal of Applied Health Communication*. https://doi.org/10.1080/00909882.2023.2179415.

Goldstein, Joseph. 2022. "Hospitals Both Strained and Essential." *New York Times*, November 20.

Goodin, Robert. 2009. "Temporal Justice." *Journal of Social Policy* 39(1): 1–16.

Goodin, Robert, James Mahmud Rice, Antti Parpo, and Lina Eriksson. 2008. *Discretionary Time: A New Measure of Freedom*. Cambridge, UK: Cambridge University Press.

Gould, E., and V. Wilson. 2020. *Black Workers Face Two of the Most Lethal Preexisting Conditions for Coronavirus—Racism and Economic Inequality*. Washington, DC: Economic Policy Institute.

Greenbaum, Susan D. 2015. *Blaming the Poor: The Long Shadow of the Moynihan Report on Cruel Images about Poverty.* New Brunswick: Rutgers University Press.

Greenhouse, Carol J. 1996. *A Moment's Notice: Time Politics across Cultures.* Ithaca: Cornell University Press.

Guendelsberger, Emily. 2019. *On the Clock: What Low-Wage Work Did to Me and How It Drives America Insane.* New York: Little, Brown.

Gupta, Akhil. 2012. *Red Tape: Bureaucracy, Structural Violence, and Poverty in India.* Durham: Duke University Press.

Hacker, Jacob S. 2006. *The Great Risk Shift: The Assault on American Jobs, Families, Health Care, and Retirement and How You Can Fight Back.* New York: Oxford University Press.

Hadley, Jack, John Holahan, Teresa Coughlin, and Dawn Miller. 2008. "Covering the Uninsured in 2008: Current Costs, Sources of Payment, and Incremental Costs." *Health Affairs* 27(Supplement 1): w399–w415. https://doi.org/10.1377/hlthaff.27.5.w399.

Halpin, Brian W., and Vicki Smith. 2017. "Employment Management Work: A Case Study and Theoretical Framework." *Work and Occupations* 44(4): 339–75.

Han, Wen-Jui, and Jake Hart. 2022. "Precarious Parental Employment, Economic Hardship, and Parenting and Child Happiness amidst a Pandemic." *Children and Youth Services Review* 133: 106343.

Harms, Erik. 2013. "Eviction Time in the New Saigon: Temporalities of Displacement in the Rubble of Development." *Cultural Anthropology* 28(2): 344–68.

Hartman, Saidiya. 2007. *Lose Your Mother: A Journey along the Atlantic Slave Route.* New York: Farrar, Straus, and Giroux.

Hefner, Jennifer L., Tory Harper Hogan, William Opoku-Agyeman, and Nir Menachemi. 2021. "Defining Safety Net Hospitals in the Health Services Research Literature: A Systematic Review and Critical Appraisal." *BMC Health Services Research* 21(1): 278. https://doi.org/10.1186/s12913-021-06292-9.

Hendren, Sara. 2020. *What Can a Body Do? How We Meet the Built Environment.* New York: Riverhead.

Henly, Julia, and Susan Lambert. 2014. "Unpredictable Work Timing in Retail Jobs: Implications for Employee Work-Life Conflict." *Industrial & Labor Relations Review* 67(3): 986–1016.

Henly, Julia, H. Luke Shaefer, and Elaine Waxman. 2006. "Nonstandard Work Schedules: Employer- and Employee-Driven Flexibility in Retail Jobs." *Social Service Review* 80(4): 609–34.

Hildebrandt, Eugenie, and Patricia Stevens. 2009. "Impoverished Women with Children and No Welfare Benefits: The Urgency of Researching Failures of the Temporary Assistance for Needy Families Program." *American Journal of Public Health* 99(5): 793–801.

Hoberman, John. 2012. *Black and Blue: The Origins and Consequences of Medical Racism.* Berkeley: University of California Press.

Hochschild, Arlie Russell. 2003. *The Managed Heart: Commercialization of Human Feeling*. Berkeley: University of California Press.
Hodgson, Dorothy L. 2011. *Gender and Culture at the Limit of Rights*. Philadelphia: University of Pennsylvania Press.
Holmes, Seth. 2013. *Fresh Fruit, Broken Bodies: Migrant Farmworkers in the United States*. Berkeley: University of California Press.
Hondagneu-Sotelo, Pierrette, and Ernestine Avila. 1997. "'I'm Here, but I'm There': The Meanings of Latina Transnational Motherhood." *Gender & Society* 11(5): 548–71.
Horton, Sarah Bronwen. 2016. *They Leave Their Kidneys in The Fields: Illness, Injury, and Illegality among US Farmworkers*. Berkeley: University of California Press.
Ingraham, Christopher. 2018. "The World's Richest Countries Guarantee Mothers More Than a Year of Paid Maternity Leave. The US Guarantees Them Nothing." *Washington Post*, February 5.
Inhorn, Marcia C. 1986. "Genital Herpes: An Ethnographic Inquiry into Being Discreditable in American Society." *Medical Anthropology Quarterly* 17(3): 39–63.
Irizarry Aponte, Claudia. 2020. "Brooklyn Woman's Death during Childbirth Spurs Renewed Outcry over Treatment Disparities." *City*, July 9.
Irwin, Neil. 2021. "Workers Are Gaining Leverage over Employers Right before Our Eyes." *New York Times*, June 5.
Jacobs, Jerry A., and Kathleen Gerson. 2004. *The Time Divide: Work, Family, and Gender Inequality*. Cambridge: Harvard University Press.
Jobson, Ryan. 2020. "The Case for Letting Anthropology Burn: Sociocultural Anthropology in 2019." *American Anthropologist* 122(2): 259–71.
Kalleberg, Arne. 2009. "Precarious Work, Insecure Workers: Employment Relations in Transition." *American Sociological Review* 74(1): 1–22.
——— . 2018. *Precarious Lives: Job Insecurity and Well-Being in Rich Democracies*. Hoboken, NJ: John Wiley.
Kantor, Jodi. 2014. "Working Anything but 9 to 5." *New York Times*, August 13.
Khafagy, Amir. 2022. "Healthcare Worker Union Is Fighting a Bill That Would End 24 Hour Shifts for Home Health Aides." *Documented*, September 13.
Kitroeff, Natalie, and Jessica Silver-Greenberg. 2019. "Pregnancy Discrimination Is Rampant inside America's Biggest Companies." *New York Times*, February 8.
Kleinman, Arthur. 2009. "Caregiving: The Odyssey of Becoming More Human." *Lancet* 373(9660): 292–93.
Knight, Kelly Ray. 2015. *Addicted. Pregnant. Poor*. Durham: Duke University Press.
Kornfeind, Katelin R., and Heather L. Sipsma. 2018. "Exploring the Link between Maternity Leave and Postpartum Depression." *Women's Health Issues* 28(4): 321–26.
Krieger, Nancy, Mary Huynh, Wenhui Li, Pamela D. Waterman, and Gretchen Van Wye. 2018. "Severe Sociopolitical Stressors and Preterm Births in New York City: 1 September 2015 to 31 August 2017." *Journal of Epidemiology and Community Health* 72(12): 1147–52.

Lambert, Susan. 2008. "Passing the Buck: Labor Flexibility Practices That Transfer Risk onto Hourly Workers." *Human Relations* 61(9): 1203–27.

Lambert, Susan, Peter Fugiel, and Julia Henly. 2014. *Precarious Work Schedules among Early-Career Employees in the US: A National Snapshot*. Chicago: Employment, Instability, Family Well-Being, and Social Policy Network, University of Chicago.

Laughlin, Lynda. 2011. *Maternity Leave and Employment Patterns of First-Time Mothers: 1961–2008*. Washington, DC: US Department of Commerce, Economics and Statistics Administration and US Census Bureau.

Lefebvre, Henri. 2004. *Rhythmanalysis: Space, Time and Everyday Life*. London: A & C Black.

Levitsky, Sandra R. 2008. "'What Rights?' The Construction of Political Claims to American Health Care Entitlements." *Law & Society Review* 42(3): 551–90.

Lewis, Tyson E. 2017. "A Marxist Education of the Encounter: Althusser, Interpellation, and the Seminar." *Rethinking Marxism* 29(2): 303–17.

Li, Jianghong, Sarah E. Johnson, Wen-Jui Han, Sonia Andrews, Garth Kendall, Lyndall Strazdins, and Alfred Dockery. 2014. "Parents' Nonstandard Work Schedules and Child Well-Being: A Critical Review of the Literature." *Journal of Primary Prevention* 35(1): 53–73.

Lohr, Steve. 2021. "Workers, in Demand, Have a New Demand of Their Own: A Career Path." *New York Times*, August 18.

Lowry, Annie. 2021. "The Time Tax." *Atlantic*, July 27.

Lu, Michael C., and Neal Halfon. 2003. "Racial and Ethnic Disparities in Birth Outcomes: A Life-Course Perspective." *Maternal and Child Health Journal* 7(1): 13–30.

Luhr, Sigrid, Daniel Schneider, and Kristen Harknett. 2022. "Parenting without Predictability: Precarious Schedules, Parental Strain, and Work-Life Conflict." *RSF: The Russell Sage Foundation Journal of the Social Sciences* 8(5): 24–44.

Macdonald, Cameron Lynne, and David A. Merrill. 2002. "'It Shouldn't Have to Be a Trade': Recognition and Redistribution in Care Work Advocacy." *Hypatia* 17(2): 67–83.

Mancini, Maggie. 2023. "Penn Residents Move to Unionize, Joining a Nationwide Trend." *Philly Voice*, February 20.

Mankekar, Purnima, and Akhil Gupta. 2019. "The Missed Period: Disjunctive Temporalities and the Work of Capital in an Indian BPO." *American Ethnologist* 46(4): 417–28.

March of Dimes. 2020. *March of Dimes Report Card*. Washington, DC: March of Dimes.

———. 2021. *Peristats: New York*. New York: March of Dimes.

Martin, Emily. 1987. *The Woman in the Body: A Cultural Analysis of Reproduction*. Boston: Beacon.

Martin, Nina, and Renee Montagne. 2017. "Black Women Keep Dying after Giving Birth. Shalon Irving's Story Tells Why." WNYC, December 7.

Martínez, Rebecca G. 2018. *Marked Women: The Cultural Politics of Cervical Cancer in Venezuela*. Stanford, CA: Stanford University Press.

Marx, Karl. (1867) 2019. *Capital*. Vol. 1. Mineola, NY: Dover.

Mas, Alexandre, and Amanda Pallais. 2017. "Valuing Alternative Work Arrangements." *American Economic Review* 107(12): 3722–59.

Massengill, Rebekah Peeples. 2013. *Wal-Mart Wars: Moral Populism in the Twenty-First Century*. New York: New York University Press.

Mauss, Marcel. (1925) 1954. *The Gift: The Form and Functions of Exchange in Archaic Societies*. New York: Free Press.

McCourt, Christine. 2013. *Childbirth, Midwifery and Concepts of Time*. New York: Berghahn.

McGrath, Maggie. 2016. "63% of Americans Don't Have Enough Savings to Cover a $500 Emergency." *Forbes*, January 6.

McIntosh, Bryan, Ronald McQuaid, Anne Munro, and Parviz Dabir-Alai. 2012. "Motherhood and Its Impact on Career Progression." *Gender in Management: An International Journal* 27(5): 346–64.

Merry, Sally Engle. 2006. "Transnational Human Rights and Local Activism: Mapping the Middle." *American Anthropologist* 108(1): 38–51.

———. 2009. *Human Rights and Gender Violence: Translating International Law into Local Justice*. Chicago: University of Chicago Press.

Miller, Amalia R. 2011. "The Effects of Motherhood Timing on Career Paths." *Journal of Population Economics* 24(3): 1071–1100.

Miller, Claire Cain, and Jim Tankersley. 2019. "Dreams of Paid Parental Leave. But Who Fits the Bill?" *New York Times*, January 8.

Mirkovic, Kelsey R., Cria G. Perrine, and Kelley S. Scanlon. 2016. "Paid Maternity Leave and Breastfeeding Outcomes." *Birth* 43(3): 233–39.

Mitchell, Lisa Meryn. 2001. *Baby's First Picture: Ultrasound and the Politics of Fetal Subjects*. Toronto: University of Toronto Press.

Mitchell, Lisa M., and Eugenia Georges. 1997. "Cross-Cultural Cyborgs: Greek and Canadian Women's Discourses on Fetal Ultrasound." *Feminist Studies* 23(2): 373–401.

Mogul, Fred. 2017. "Black Mothers Face Higher Complication Rates When Delivering Babies in NYC." *WNYC News*, January 16.

Mol, Annemarie. 2008. *The Logic of Care: Health and the Problem of Patient Choice*: New York: Routledge.

Morgan, Lynn M., and Elizabeth F. S. Roberts. 2012. "Reproductive Governance in Latin America." *Anthropology & Medicine* 19(2): 241–54. https://doi.org/10.1080/13648470.2012.675046.

Muehlebach, Andrea. 2012. *The Moral Neoliberal: Welfare and Citizenship in Italy*. Chicago: University of Chicago Press.

Mulla, Sameena. 2014. *The Violence of Care*. New York: New York University Press.
Mulligan, Jessica M. 2017. "Segmented Risks: Eligibility and Resentment on Insurance Exchanges." In *Unequal Coverage: The Experience of Health Care Reform in the United States*, edited by Jessica M. Mulligan and Heide Castañeda, 132–55. New York: New York University Press.
Mullings, Leith. 2005. "Resistance and Resilience: The Sojourner Syndrome and the Social Context of Reproduction in Central Harlem." *Transforming Anthropology* 12(2): 79–91.
Mullings, Leith, and Alaka Wali. 2001. *Stress and Resilience: The Social Context of Reproduction in Central Harlem*. Secaucus, NJ: Springer Science & Business Media.
Munn, Nancy. 1992. "The Cultural Anthropology of Time: A Critical Essay." *Annual Review of Anthropology* 21:93–123.
Murphy, Michelle. 2017. *The Economization of Life*. Durham: Duke University Press.
Nanni, Giordano. 2017. *The Colonization of Time: Ritual, Routine, and Resistance in the British Empire*. Manchester, UK: Manchester University Press.
National Women's Law Center. 2014. *Underpaid and Overloaded: Women in Low-Wage Jobs*. Washington, DC: National Women's Law Center.
Nelson, Maggie. 2015. *The Argonauts*. Minneapolis: Greywolf.
Newman, Katherine S. 2009. *No Shame in My Game: The Working Poor in the Inner City*. New York: Vintage.
New York City Bureau of Vital Statistics. 2021. *Summary of Vital Statistics 2018: The City of New York*. New York: New York City Department of Health and Mental Hygiene.
New York City Commission on Human Rights. 2021. "Legal Enforcement Guidance on Discrimination on the Basis of Pregnancy, Childbirth, Related Medical Conditions, Lactation Accommodations, and Sexual or Reproductive Health Decisions."
New York City Department of Health and Mental Hygiene. 2015. *Pregnancy-Associated Mortality, New York City, 2006–2010*. New York: New York City Department of Health and Mental Hygiene.
———. 2016. *Severe Maternal Morbidity in New York City, 2008–2012*. New York: New York City Department of Health and Mental Hygiene.
New York State. 2022. "Ahead of Father's Day, Governor Hochul Announces Record Number of New York Fathers Used Nation Leading Paid Family Leave Program in 2021." Press Office of Governor Hochul. www.governor.ny.gov.
New York State Department of Health. 2013. "Percent Early and Late or No Prenatal Care, by Race and Resident County, New York State—2013." www.health.ny.gov.
Niles, P. Mimi, Ifeyinwa V. Asiodu, Joia Crear-Perry, Zoë Julian, Audrey Lyndon, Monica R. McLemore, Arianna M. Planey, Karen A. Scott, and Saraswathi Vedam. 2020. "Reflecting on Equity in Perinatal Care during a Pandemic." *Health Equity* 4(1): 330–33.

Niles, Paulomi Mimi, Saraswathi Vedam, Amy Witkoski Stimpfel, and Allison Squires. 2021. "Kairos Care in a Chronos World: Midwifery Care as Model of Resistance and Accountability in Public Health Settings." *Birth* 48(4): 480–92.
NPR, Robert W. Johnson Foundation, and T. H. Chan School of Public Health. 2020. *The Impact of Coronavirus on Households, by Race/Ethnicity*. New York: National Public Radio, Robert W. Johnson Foundation, and T. H. Chan School of Public Health.
Odell, Jenny. 2023. *Saving Time: Discovering a Life beyond the Clock*. New York: Random House.
O'Neill, Bruce. 2017. *The Space of Boredom: Homelessness in the Slowing Global Order*. Durham: Duke University Press.
Opdycke, Sandra. 1999. *No One Was Turned Away: The Role of Public Hospitals in New York City since 1900*. New York: Oxford University Press.
Oshinsky, David. 2016. *Bellevue: Three Centuries of Medicine and Mayhem at America's Most Storied Hospital*. New York: Doubleday.
Pande, Amrita. 2014. *Wombs in Labor: Transnational Commercial Surrogacy in India*. New York: Columbia University Press.
Paquette, Danielle. 2015. "The Shocking Number of New Moms Who Return to Work Two Weeks after Childbirth." *Washington Post*, August 19.
Parreñas, Rhacel Salazar. 2005. *Children of Global Migration: Transnational Families and Gendered Woes*. Palo Alto, CA: Stanford University Press.
Phillips-Fein, Kim. 2017. *Fear City: New York's Fiscal Crisis and the Rise of Austerity Politics*. New York: Metropolitan Books.
Pihl, Ariel Marek, and Gaetano Basso. 2019. "Did California Paid Family Leave Impact Infant Health?" *Journal of Policy Analysis and Management* 38(1): 155–80.
Porter, Eduardo. 2021. "Low-Wage Workers Now Have Options, Which Could Mean a Raise." *New York Times*, July 20.
Presser, Harriet B. 2003. *Working in a 24/7 Economy: Challenges for American Families*. New York: Russell Sage Foundation.
Presser, Harriet, and Brian Ward. 2011. "Nonstandard Work Schedules over the Life Course: A First Look." *Monthly Labor Review* 134(7): 3–16.
Puig de la Bellacasa, María. 2017. *Matters of Care: Speculative Ethics in More Than Human Worlds*. Minneapolis: University of Minnesota Press.
Ragoné, Helena. 1994. *Surrogate Motherhood: Conception in the Heart*. Boulder, CO: Westview.
Ransom, Jan. 2018. "City's New Public Hospitals Chief Will Focus on Primary Care." *New York Times*, January 7.
Ray, Ranita. 2018. *The Making of a Teenage Service Class: Poverty and Mobility in an American City*. Berkeley: University of California Press.
Roberts, Dorothy. 1997. *Killing the Black Body: Race, Reproduction, and the Meaning of Liberty*. New York: Pantheon.

Robertson, Campbell, and Robert Gebeloff. 2020. "How Millions of Women Became the Most Essential Workers in America." *New York Times*, April 8.

Rollins, Judith. 1985. *Between Women: Domestics and Their Employers*. Philadelphia: Temple University Press.

Rose, Nikolas. 2007. *The Politics of Life Itself: Biomedicine, Power, and Subjectivity in the Twenty-First Century*. Princeton: Princeton University Press.

Rosenbaum, Susanna. 2017. *Domestic Economies: Women, Work, and the American Dream in Los Angeles*. Durham: Duke University Press.

Rosenthal, Caitlin. 2018. *Accounting for Slavery: Masters and Management*. Cambridge: Harvard University Press.

Ross, Loretta, and Rickie Solinger. 2017. *Reproductive Justice: An Introduction*. Berkeley: University of California Press.

Ross, Martha, and Nicole Bateman. 2019. *Meet the Low Wage Workforce*. Washington, DC: Brookings Institute.

Sassen, Saskia. 1999. *Globalization and Its Discontents: Essays on the New Mobility of People and Money*. New York: New Press.

Saunders, Barry F. 2010. *CT Suite: The Work of Diagnosis in the Age of Noninvasive Cutting*. Durham: Duke University Press.

Scheiber, Noam. 2015. "The Perils of Ever-Changing Work Schedules to Children's Well-Being." *New York Times*, August 12.

———. 2022. "Despite Labor Shortages, Workers See Few Gains in Economic Security." *New York Times*, February 1.

Scheper-Hughes, Nancy. 1993. *Death without Weeping: The Violence of Everyday Life in Brazil*. Berkeley: University of California Press.

Schneider, Daniel, and Kristen Harknett. 2019. "Consequences of Routine Work-Schedule Instability for Worker Health and Well-Being." *American Sociological Review* 84(1): 82–114.

———. 2022. "Maternal Exposure to Work Schedule Unpredictability and Child Behavior." *Journal of Marriage and Family* 84(1): 187–209.

Schwartz, Barry. 1974. "Waiting, Exchange, and Power: The Distribution of Time in Social Systems." *American Journal of Sociology* 79(4): 841–70.

Sharma, Sarah. 2014. *In the Meantime: Temporality and Cultural Politics*. Durham: Duke University Press.

Silver-Greenberg, Jessica, and Natalie Kitroeff. 2018. "Miscarrying at Work: The Physical Toll of Pregnancy Discrimination." *New York Times*, October 21.

Singer, Elyse Ona. 2022. *Lawful Sins: Abortion Rights and Reproductive Governance in Mexico*. Palo Alto, CA: Stanford University Press.

Slaughter, Anne-Marie. 2013. "How to Make the US a Better Place for Caregivers." *Atlantic*, May 14.

Smialek, Jeanna. 2021. "Powell Says Better Child Care Policies Might Lift Women in Workforce." *New York Times*, February 27.

Smith-Oka, Vania. 2009. "Unintended Consequences: Exploring the Tensions between Development Programs and Indigenous Women in Mexico in the Context of Reproductive Health." *Social Science & Medicine* 68(11): 2069–77.

Snyder, Benjamin H. 2016. *The Disrupted Workplace: Time and the Moral Order of Flexible Capitalism*. Oxford, UK: Oxford University Press.

Span, Paula. 2021. "For Older Adults, Home Care Has Become Harder to Find." *New York Times*, July 24.

Standing, Guy. 2014. *A Precariat Charter: From Denizens to Citizens*. London: A & C Black.

Stevenson, Lisa. 2014. *Life beside Itself: Imagining Care in the Canadian Arctic*. Berkeley: University of California Press.

Strong, Adrienne. 2020. *Documenting Death: Maternal Mortality and the Ethics of Care in Tanzania*. Berkeley: University of California Press.

Stuesse, Angela. 2016. *Scratching Out a Living: Latinos, Race, and Work in the Deep South*. Berkeley: University of California Press.

Sufrin, Carolyn. 2017. *Jailcare: Finding the Safety Net for Women behind Bars*. Berkeley: University of California Press.

Thompson, Edward P. 1967. "Time, Work-Discipline, and Industrial Capitalism." *Past & Present* 38:56–97.

Ticktin, Miriam. 2011. *Casualties of Care: Immigration and the Politics of Humanitarianism in France*. Berkeley: University of California Press.

Toossi, Mitra. 2002. "A Century of Change: The US Labor Force, 1950–2050." *Monthly Labor Review* 125(5): 15–28.

Torres, Felipe. 2021. *Temporal Regimes: Materiality, Politics, Technology*. New York: Routledge.

Tsing, Anna. 2015. *The Mushroom at the End of the World: On the Possibility of Life in Capitalist Ruins*. Princeton: Princeton University Press.

Villarosa, Linda. 2018. "Why America's Black Mothers and Babies Are in a Life-or-Death Crisis." *New York Times Magazine*, April 11.

Wacquant, Loïc. 2009. *Punishing the Poor: The Neoliberal Government of Social Insecurity*. Durham: Duke University Press.

Waggoner, Miranda. 2017. *The Zero Trimester: Pre-Pregnancy Care and the Politics of Reproductive Risk*. Berkeley: University of California Press.

Waldman, Annie. 2017. "How Hospitals Are Failing Black Mothers." *ProPublica*, December 27.

Weeks, Kathi. 2011. *The Problem with Work: Feminism, Marxism, Antiwork Politics, and Postwork Imaginaries*. Durham: Duke University Press.

Willen, Sarah. 2012. "Migration, 'Illegality,' and Health: Mapping Embodied Vulnerability and Debating Health-Related Deservingness." *Social Science & Medicine* 74(6): 805–11.

Williams, Joan. 2001. *Unbending Gender: Why Family and Work Conflict and What to Do about It*. Oxford, UK: Oxford University Press.

———. 2006. *One Sick Child Away from Being Fired: When "Opting Out" Is Not an Option*. San Francisco: Hastings College of the Law.

Williams, Joan C., Mary Blair-Loy, and Jennifer L. Berdahl. 2013. "Cultural Schemas, Social Class, and the Flexibility Stigma." *Journal of Social Issues* 69(2): 209–34.

Winant, Gabriel. 2021. *The Next Shift*. Cambridge: Harvard University Press.

Zerubavel, Eviatar. 1979. *Patterns of Time in Hospital Life: A Sociological Perspective*. Chicago: University of Chicago Press.

Zimmerman, Mary K., Jacquelyn S. Litt, and Christine E. Bose. 2006. *Global Dimensions of Gender and Carework*. Stanford, CA: Stanford University Press.

Zundl, Elaine, Daniel Schneider, Kristen Harknett, and Evelyn Bellew. 2022. "Still Unstable: The Persistence of Schedule Uncertainty during the Pandemic." Shift Project Research Brief, Harvard University. https://shift.hks.harvard.edu.

INDEX

abortion, 162–63
accommodations, pregnancy-related, 26–27; care and, 30, 85, 93–94; personalism influencing, 135–36; PWFA requiring, 18, 71, 129; within rights, 131–32; supervisors and, 49, 125; workers not asking about, 125
administrators, at Beaumont Hospital, 115–16
affective care, care work contrasted with, 146
affective labor, 34
Affordable Care Act, 17, 172n2
afterlife of slavery, 11, 50, 65
aides. *See* home health aides
American Rescue Plan Act, 160
annual income, 25–26
appointments, prenatal. *See* prenatal appointments
attendance policies, 48, 158
Auguste, Yvonne (service worker), 119–20, 127–30

Baron, Cintia (union organizaer), 46, 55, 138–42
Beaumont Hospital (pseudonym), 1, 22, 102; administrators at, 115–16; demographics of population of, 25; interviews at, 27; obstetrics department conditions at, 95, 112–13, 156–57; prenatal care at, 26; schedules accommodated by, 105; temporal governance at, 83, 90, 103–5; waiting at, 95, 100; walk-in patients eliminated by, 90–91. *See also* prenatal clinic

Dr. Becker (administrator), 111, 114
A Better Balance (organization), 131
Bharadwaj, Aditya, 24
Black and brown women: as caregivers, 33; as low-wage workers, 11; medical neglect experienced by, 154; reproductive health disparities and, 15–21, 154–55; service work and, 74
Black infant mortality rates, 15–16
de Blasio, Bill, 99
Bourgois, Philippe, 106–7
Braxton-Hicks contractions, 48
Brodwin, Paul, 114
Brooklyn, in New York City, 25, 62, 132; private doctors' offices lacking in, 98–99; safety net hospitals in, 16; temporal labor flow in, 33. *See also* Beaumont Hospital
brown women. *See* Black and brown women
Buch, Elana, 34–35
bureaucratic time, at safety net public prenatal clinic, 83
burnout, at safety net hospitals, 113
Ms. Butler (nurse-practitioner), 112–13, 114–15

call-outs, from work, 41, 43, 47, 50
care, 149; accommodations interpreted as, 30, 93–94; affective, 146; under COVID-19 pandemic, 151–53; definition of, 121; de-gendering of, 144; employers framed through, 131–35; ethics of, 115; expectations of, 135–37; experiences of, 150; failures of, 106–10;

care (*cont.*)
　maternal, 92; personalist interpretive frameworks and, 131–32; reproductive, 155; rights contrasted with, 131–32, 148; time and personalism and, 135–37. *See also* prenatal care
caregivers, 33, 133
caregiving, cultural beliefs about, 34, 143
care labor, mass incarceration paralleling, 49–50
care work, 131–32, 145; affective care contrasted with, 146; by female labor force, 10; inequalities in, 9, 152
cashiers, 85
Chamberlain, Jayda (service worker), 71
childcare, 156
Clawson, Dan, 43, 89
clinic, prenatal. *See* prenatal clinic
clinical time, 14, 19–20, 117, 171n2; inequalities shaping, 113; labor time and, 85, 107; negative states produced by, 109–10; safety net prenatal care shaped by, 97
"clock time," industrial, 18–19
clopening (shift), 37–38, 157–58
Colen, Shellee, 6
Commission on Human Rights, of New York City, 122, 128
communities of color: reproductive care in, 155; safety net health institutions serving, 96; temporal regimes subordinating, 110
complaint process, against supervisors, 122–23, 126
contractions, Braxton-Hicks, 48
contracts, pacts differentiated from, 136
Cooper, Amy, 107
Cooper, Melinda, 68
COVID-19 pandemic, 21, 31; care under, 151–53; inequalities exacerbated by, 153, 155; New York City impacted by, 29, 151–52; reproductive health disparities exacerbated by, 154–55; stratified reproduction exacerbated by, 152
co-workers, relationships with, 86–90

death, maternal, 154
desk jobs, aspiring to, 75–82
developing countries, foreign companies moving to, 8
discipline, time. *See* time discipline
discrimination, 128; gender, 129; in healthcare, 97–100; housing, 98, 171n1; New York City defining, 130; pregnancy, 59, 80–81, 122, 129–30; racial, 171n1
Dobbs vs Jackson Women's Health Organization (Supreme Court decision), 163
doctors, 101–2, 112
doctor's note, call-outs excused through, 50
dog whistle politics, 98
"double freedom," of workers, 50–51

Earned Sick Time Act (New York City), 3
"economization of life," 98
employees, part time, 2, 44–46
employers, 18, 157–58; care framing, 131–35; labor time controlled by, 46; pace of work intensified by, 74; rights information required to be displayed by, 123; scheduling software used by, 40, 45; service, 13, 44, 46; workers' time controlled by, 47, 93
essential workers, 152
ethics of care, temporal regimes challenging, 115
ethnic succession, 60–64
everyday ethics, 114

failures of care, time seizures and, 106–10
Fair Workweek Law (New York City), 157–58, *159*

Family and Medical Leave Act (FMLA), 35, 54; eligibility of, 55–56; ideologies embedded in, 59; PFLA contrasted with, 146
family configurations, diverse, 144
family leave, paid. *See* paid leave
fatigue, at work, 69–70
federal legislation, low-wage workers lacking, 44–45
female labor force, 10
#FightforFifteen, 157
Fletcher, Abigail (service worker), 91
flexible labor, 12–15
"flex-work" policies, 13
Floyd, George, 153
FMLA. *See* Family and Medical Leave Act
food stamps, 140–41, 171n7
foreign companies, developing countries moved to by, 8
Fraser, Vanessa (service worker), 40–41

GDP. *See* Gross Domestic Product
gendered labor: reorganization of, 144; service work and, 9–11, 24
Georges, Sabrina (service worker), 47, 76, 158
Germaine, Lucia (service worker), 41–42, 73, 84, 92, 125
Gerstel, Naomi, 43, 89
gestational time, 14–15, 19–20, 66, 171n4; labor time contrasted with, 67–74; time discipline conflicting with, 30; in vivo, 71, 81
Glaser, Alana, 130
governance, temporal. *See* temporal governance
Great Risk Shift, 8
Greene, Tammy (service worker), 125
Gross Domestic Product (GDP), service sector dominating, 7
Gupta, Akhil, 93

gynecology department, at Beaumont Hospital, 156–57

Hartman, Saidiya, 11
Ms. Hayworth (receptionist), 100, 106
health, of pregnancy, 75
health aides. *See* home health aides
healthcare sector, temporal precarity in, 41–42
healthcare system, public, 97–99
health disparities, reproductive. *See* reproductive health disparities
health insurance, 22, 26
Ms. Hernández (receptionist), 63
hierarchies of labor, racial, 78
Hochul, Kathy, 156, 157–58
Holmes, Seth, 78
home health aides, 71, 74, 83–84, 119, 158; advertisements for, 62; pregnancies limiting ability to fulfill tasks of, 72–73; temporal precarity impacting, 42; without paid leave, 138–40
homelessness, 127
hospitals, safety net. *See* safety net hospitals
hourly-wage workers, 39
hours, insufficient, 44–45
human rights, 128–31
hunger, at work, 69–70

IMF. *See* International Monetary Fund
incarceration, mass, 49–50
income: annual, 25–26; inequalities in, 58–59; loss of, 3, 10, 13, 18, 83, 92; paid leave reducing, 146; prenatal care prioritized by, 91; of working-class families, 9–10. *See also* low-income women
industrial "clock time," service workers' wages connected to, 18–19
Industrial Revolution, time discipline influenced by, 68–69

inequalities: in care work, 9; clinical time shaped by, 113; COVID-19 pandemic exacerbating, 153, 155; in income, 58–59; low-income women facing, 103–4; in maternal health, 15–17, 99, 154; PFLA embedded with, 146; within policy, 52–60; prenatal clinic reproducing, 110; racial, 97–99, 153–54; reproductive temporalities and, 39–40, 153; structural, 115–16; temporal, 15–21; temporal governance intertwined with, 6, 103–5; temporal regimes reproducing, 117
infant mortality rates, Black, 15–16
inflation, low-income families impacted by, 161–62
insufficient hours, at work, 44–45
insurance, health, 22, 26
International Monetary Fund (IMF), 8
interpretive frameworks, personalist, 131–34
interviews, at Beaumont Hospital (pseudonym), 27

Joanna (midwife), 104, 113
Johnson, Michaela (service worker), 65, 74, 82, 86, 113, 134–36
Jones, Nyanna (service worker), 53, 56, 91
Ms. Jones (patient care associate), 115
Joseph, Mary-Ann (service worker), 1–2, 6, 39, 46–47
justice, temporal, 137–43, 148, 151

Knight, Kelly Ray, 171n4

labor, at work: affective, 34; care, 49–50; changing landscape of, 157–62; flexible, 12–15; gendered, 144; hierarchies of, 78; reproductive, 34–35; temporal, 33. *See also* temporal genes: service labor
labor force, female, 10

labor market, 161
labor participation, female, 9
Labor Relations Department, of New York City, 122
labor system, penal system contrasted with, 48
labor time, 14, 19–20; clinical time and, 85, 107; employers controlling, 46; gestational time contrasted with, 67–74; prenatal care shaped by, 67; in service work, 35–44
labor time, loss of, 58
Lambert, Susan, 38
Latinx women. *See* Black and brown women
laziness, discourses of, 81–82
leave, paid. *See* paid leave
Louis, Stéphanie (service worker), 42, 84
low-income families, inflation impacting, 161–62
low-income people, temporal regimes subordinating, 110
low-income pregnant working people, safety net programs for, 17–18
low-income women: inequalities faced by, 103–4; prenatal care lacked by, 20; reproductive time of, 59
low-wage service employees, empowerment of, 161
low-wage workers, 3–4, 56, 157; Black and brown women as, 11; definition of, 10; federal legislation lacked for, 44–45; Paid Safe and Sick Leave Act and, 53; pregnancies lost by, 76–77; temporal precarity impacting, 13; 24/7 service economy impacting, 12; vulnerability continuing for, 53–54

mailing address, complaint process relying on, 127–28
Mailler, Jenae (service worker), 85
Mankekar, Purnima, 93

manufacturing sector, 7–8
Martínez, Mariel (service worker), 37, 43
Marx, Karl, 51, 74
Mason, Angela (policy advocate), 60
Mason, Cleo (service worker), 102–3
mass incarceration, 49–50
maternal death, 154
maternal mortality rates, 15–16
Mauss, Marcel, 89
Medicaid (insurance), 26; eligibility for, 17, 141–42, 172n2; New York State expansion of, 17–18, 156; participants covered by, 26; prenatal screening required for, 103
medical neglect, Black and brown women experiencing, 154
medical practice, racism in, 96–97
midwives, doctors contrasted with, 112
minimum wage, 37, 157
miscarriages, 75–77
Morgan, Lynn, 17
mortality rates, 15–16
motherhood, ideologies of, 75–76, 92–93
mothers, single, 36
Muehlebach, Andrea, 135
Murphy, Michelle, 98

National Partnership for Women and Families, 161
nausea, from pregnancy at work, 36
neglect, medical, 154
New York City, 1, *124*, 172n3; Bronx in, 25; Commission on Human Rights of, 122, 128; COVID-19 pandemic impacting, 29, 151–52; discrimination as defined by, 130; Earned Sick Time Act in, 3; Fair Workweek Law in, 157–58, *159*; Labor Relations Department of, 122; local, state, and national policy in, 21–22; prenatal care providers in, 27–28; public healthcare system of, 97–99; rental and housing prices in, 126–27; reproductive health disparities in, 15–21; safety net programs in, 17. *See also* Brooklyn; Paid Safe and Sick Leave Act; Paid Sick Leave Law; Pregnant Workers Fairness Act
New York City Council, 158
New York State, 17–18, 28–29, 156. *See also* Paid Family Leave Act
"No More 24" (proposed bill), 158
nonstandard schedules, 39–41, 84
nurses, public hospital threatened with strikes by, 172n3

obstetrics department, at Beaumont Hospital, 112–13, 156–57
offices, of private doctors, 98–99
#OurTimeCounts, 158

pacts, contracts differentiated from, 136
Paid Family Leave Act (PFLA), 28–29, 31, 52, 137, 140–43, 147–48; advocacy materials for, 139; billboards advertising, 144; FMLA contrasted with, 146; inequalities embedded in, 146; lobbying for, 138; publicity campaigns for, *145*; PWFA contrasted with, 121; reproductive time re-valued by, 145; roll out of, 155
paid leave, 53, 57, 160; advocating for, 142–47; home health aides without, 138–40; income reduced during, 146; United States without, 54
Paid Safe and Sick Leave Act (New York City), 17, 24, 26, 30–31, 60; amendments to, 171n1; low-wage workers and, 53; policy landscape reshaped by, 120
Paid Sick Leave Law (New York City), 3, 17, 171n1
pandemic, COVID. *See* COVID-19 pandemic
part time employees, 2, 44–46

patient care associates (PCAs), 102
penal system, labor system contrasted with, 48
Persaud, Dana (service worker), 108
personalism, 148; accommodations influenced by, 135–36; gendered impacts of, 137; time and expectations of care and, 135–37
personalist interpretive frameworks, 131–34
personal protective equipment (PPE), 152
PFLA. *See* Paid Family Leave Act
Phillips, Shanelle (service worker), 135
physical labor, status and, 78
policies, attendance, 41, 48, 158
policies, "flex-work," 13
policy, related to pregnancy at work: changing landscape of, 157–62; inequalities within, 52–60; stratified reproduction amplified by, 58. *See also* Family and Medical Leave Act; Paid Family Leave Act; Paid Safe and Sick Leave Act; Pregnant Workers Fairness Act
"politics of disclosure," service workers impacted by, 89–90
politics of value, temporal justice and, 137–43
postpartum depression, 138–40, 141
PPD. *See* purified protein derivative
PPE. *See* personal protective equipment
precarious work, service sector exemplifying, 11
precarity, schedule. *See* schedule precarity
precarity, temporal. *See* temporal precarity
pregnancy. *See specific topics*
Pregnancy Discrimination Act (1978), 52, 129
Pregnant Workers Fairness Act (PWFA), 3, 24, 26, 30–31, 52, 60; accommodations required under, 18, 71, 129; Commission on Human Rights dealing with, 128; PFLA contrasted with, 121; policy landscape reshaped by, 120; poster publicizing, 79; Pregnancy Discrimination Act contrasted with, 129; rights and, 122–31; states passing, 160; state version of, 172n3; supervisors ignoring, 71; systems of value reproduced by, 35; workers doubting value of, 126
prenatal appointments, 88; assigning of, 83–86, 104; legal right to time for, 91; work schedules in conflict with, 2–3, 19, 83–86, 90–93
prenatal care, 2–3, 15–18, 21, 84; access to, 5, 27–28; at Beaumont Hospital (pseudonym), 26; income not prioritized over, 91; labor time shaping, 67; late, 19–20; low-income women lacking, 20; schedules impacting, 88–89; temporal governance of, 93; work conflicting with, 90–93. *See also* safety net prenatal care; waiting, during prenatal care
prenatal care providers, in New York City, 27–28
prenatal clinic, at Beaumont Hospital, 29; inequalities reproduced by, 110; temporal governance at, 100–105; temporal regimes at, 108; waiting room of, 23–24
prenatal screening, Medicaid requiring, 103, 106
Presser, Harriet, 39
preterm labor, during pregnancy, 48
private doctors'offices, 98–99
professional occupations, pregnancy in, 80
public health, "racist neoliberalism" influencing, 99
public healthcare system, of New York City, 97–99

public hospital, nurses threatening to strike at, 172n3
Puig de la Bellacasa, María, 163
PUMP for Nursing Mothers (bill), 160
purified protein derivative (PPD), 95
PWFA. *See* Pregnant Workers Fairness Act

racism, in medical practice, 96–97
"racist neoliberalism," public health influenced by, 99
redlining, 98, 171n1
regimes, temporal. *See* temporal regimes
rental and housing prices, in New York City, 126–27
reproduction, stratified. *See* stratified reproduction
reproductive care, in communities of color, 15–17, 97–100, 155
reproductive governance, 17; temporal governance in relation to, 162–63
reproductive health disparities: COVID-19 pandemic exacerbating, 154–55; in New York City, 15–21; stratified reproduction and, 153–54. *See also* stratified reproduction
reproductive labor, gender and racial stereotypes in, 34–35
reproductive risk, service work and, 75–79
reproductive temporalities, 5, 146; inequalities in, 39–40, 153; nonstandard schedules compounding, 39–40; service work producing, 5; temporal governance shaping, 57, 149; temporal regimes constraining, 63
reproductive time, 81; of low-income women, 59; PFLA re-valuing, 145; re-valuing of, 143–47
respect, discourse of, 106
restaurant, work at, 70
retail workers, 2, 40–41, 53, 56, 65, 69, 86

Ms. Richards (midwife), 115
rights, 120; accommodations within, 131–32; billboard promoting, *124*; care contrasted with, 131–32, 148; employers required to display information on, 123; human, 128–31; law requiring display of information on, 123–25; obstacles to claiming, 123; PWFA and, 122–31; supervisors violating, 128. *See also* human rights
Robbins, Katherine Gallagher (service worker), 161
Roberts, Elizabeth, 17
Robinson, Maureen (service worker), 88
Rollins, Judith, 131–32

safety net healthcare system, as broken, 115
safety net health institutions: communities of color served by, 96; during COVID-19, 154; disinvestment into, 96–99; temporal regimes of, 21; waiting at, 5, 100
safety net hospitals, 1, 22; in Brooklyn, 16; burnout at, 113; private doctors' offices and, 98–99; reimbursement of, 172n2; wait times at, 102–3. *See also* Beaumont Hospital
safety net prenatal care: clinical time shaping, 97; temporal regimes of, 66, 149; waiting during, 100, 108
safety net programs, 17–18
safety net public prenatal clinic, bureaucratic time at, 83
safety net services, service workers depending on, 19
St Jean, Lovelie (service worker), 72–73, 81
Sartre, Jean-Paul, 61
Sassen, Saskia, 10
Saunders, Barry, 111
schedule precarity, 38

schedules, for work: Beaumont Hospital accommodating, 105; corporations auditing, 46–47; nonstandard, 39–41, 84; prenatal appointments in conflict with, 2–3, 86, 90; prenatal care impacted by, 88–89; temporal precarity caused by, 85; unpredictability of, 2, 40, 158
screening, prenatal, 103
service sector, 68; GDP dominated by, 7; nonstandard schedules in, 40–41; precarious work exemplified by, 11; race, class and gender in, 7–11; temporal governance of, 69; time in, 1, 38–40
service work: Black and brown women and, 74; desk job contrasted with, 77; by female labor force, 10; gender and racial stereotypes in, 34–35; history of, 7–12; labor time in, 35–44; personalist interpretive frameworks in, 132; pregnancy impacted by, 76–77; reproductive temporalities produced by, 5; temporal precarity in, 35–44; temporal regimes of, 43, 66, 148; women of color overrepresented in, 11
service workers, 40–41, 53, 146–47; "the politics of disclosure" impacting, 89–90; punitive labor practices against, 87–88; safety net services depended on by, 19; temporal precarity of, 44, 52
service workplaces: low-wage, 21, 35; temporal governance of, 50–51; temporal regimes of, 21, 63–64
settler colonialism, reproductive disparities influenced by, 16–17
Sharma, Sarah, 44
shifts, swapping, 89
sick leave, paid. *See* paid leave
Dr. Silva (doctor), 22, 90, 114
Singh, Marlia (service worker), 83
single mothers, 36
Slaughter, Ann-Marie, 144

slavery: afterlife of, 11, 50, 65; reproductive disparities influenced by, 16–17; time discipline rooted in, 69
Smith, Jerusha (service worker), 50, 60
Smith, Nadia (service worker), 45, 77
Smith, Nicola (service worker), 132–34
Snyder, Benjamin, 14, 50
Special Supplemental Nutrition Program for Women, Infants and Children (WIC), 26, 171n6
Standing, Guy, 11, 45
status: physical labor and, 78; temporal governance and, 105–6; waiting and, 102
stratified reproduction: COVID-19 pandemic exacerbating, 152; policy amplifying, 58; time and, 6
Stuesse, Angela, 45
succession, ethnic, refusal of reform and, 60–64
supervisors, 47–48, 72, 76, 94, 134–35; accommodations and, 49, 125; Auguste in conflict with, 119–20, 129–30; complaint process against, 122–23, 126; health care aides not penalized by, 84; pregnancy not sympathized with by, 3; PWFA ignored by, 71; relationships with, 86–90; rights violated by, 128; temporal governance impacting, 49; temporal regimes produced through, 67; Temporary Disability Insurance not filed for by, 140
Supplemental Nutrition Assistance Program "food stamps," 171n7
Supreme Court, US, 162–63, 172n2
surrogacy, work time and, 67–68
swapping shifts, 89

Taylor, Clarice (service worker), 77, 108
Taylor, Frederick Winslow, 68
temporal governance, 4, 14–15, 18–20, 26, 29, 35, 44–46; at Beaumont Hospital,

83, 90; definition of, 4; inequalities intertwined with, 6, 103–5; of prenatal care, 93; at prenatal clinic, 100–105; reproductive governance in relation to, 162–63; reproductive temporalities shaped by, 57, 149; of service sector, 69; of service workplaces, 50–51; state power to rein in, 157–58; status and, 105–6; supervisors impacted by, 49; temporal precarity caused by, 13, 63; time devalued through, 6; unpaid time rewarded by, 47

temporalities, reproductive. *See* reproductive temporalities

temporal justice, 137–43, 148, 151

temporal labor flow, 33

temporal precarity, 12–15, 142; in healthcare sector, 41–42; home health aides impacted by, 42; low-wage workers impacted by, 13; schedules causing, 85; in service work, 35–44; of service workers, 52; temporal governance caused by, 13, 63

temporal regimes, 4, 6, 26, 37, 87; communities of color subordinated by, 110; ethics of care challenged by, 115; inequalities reproduced by, 117; low-income people subordinated by, 110; at prenatal clinic, 108; reproductive temporalities constrained by, 63; of safety net health institutions, 21; of safety net prenatal care, 66, 149; of regimes, 66; of service work, 43, 148; of service workplaces, 21, 63–64; supervisors producing, 67; time wasted by, 108; waiting created by, 109

Temporary Disability Insurance, 138, 140, 146

Thomas, Ayesha (service worker), 75, 125

Thompson, E. P., 68

three strikes (absence policy), 47–48

Ticktin, Miriam, 128

time, of workers, 52, 83; of doctors, 101–2; employers controlling, 47, 93; personalism and expectations of care and, 135–37; in service sector, 1; stratified reproduction and, 6; temporal governance devaluing, 6; temporal regimes wasting, 108; unpaid, 45, 47; value of, 44–50, 157. *See also* clinical time; gestational time; labor time; reproductive time

time, unpaid, 45, 47

time discipline, 68–71, 93; collective life constituted out of, 162; gestational time conflicting with, 30; health impacted by, 75; Industrial Revolution producing, 68–69; slavery as root of, 69

time seizures, failures of care and, 106–10

time urgency, everyday ethics conflicting with, 114

Tompkins, Shanelle (service worker), 92, 108, 113

translation, of human rights, 129–30

travel, to work, 46, 140

Tremain, Jasmine (service worker), 50, 69, 107–8

underemployment, 44, 46

uninsured patients, 22–23

union employee, work as, 142

United States: maternal mortality rates in, 15; Supreme Court of, 162–63, 172n2; without paid leave, 54. *See also* New York City

unpaid time, 45, 47

unpredictability, of schedules, 2

value, politics of, 137–43

"vocabulary of virtue," 136

wages, 8; industrial "clock time" connected to, 18–19; minimum, 37, 157; pregnancy and lost, 52–53. *See also* income

waiting, during prenatal care, 97, 100, 103–5, 110–11; at Beaumont Hospital, 95; economic cost of, 106; inequality and, 106–9; poor people forced into, 101; at safety net health institutions, 5; during safety net prenatal care, 108; status and, 102; temporal regimes creating, 109
wait times, at safety net hospitals, 102–3
Waldby, Catherine, 68
Walker, Michelle (service worker), 84–85
walk-in patients, Beaumont Hospital eliminating, 90–91
Washington, Sha-Asia, 154
Washington, Tasha (service worker), 70, 77–78, 88–89
"welfare-to-work" amendments (1996), 10
Willen, Sarah, 136
Williams, Tanisha (service worker), 35–36, 43
Winant, Gabriel, 162
women, Black and brown. *See* Black and brown women
women, low-income. *See* low-income women
women of color, service work overrepresented in by, 11
work. *See specific topics*
workers: "double freedom" of, 50–51; essential, 152; hourly-wage, 39; PWFA doubted by, 126; retail, 2, 40–41, 53, 56, 69, 86; undocumented, 17, 26, 125, 153. *See also* home health aides; low-wage workers; service workers
working-class families, income of, 9–10
workplaces, service. *See* service workplaces
work time, surrogacy and, 67–68
World Bank, 8

ABOUT THE AUTHOR

ELISE ANDAYA is Associate Professor of Anthropology at the University at Albany (State University of New York). Her previous book, *Conceiving Cuba: Reproduction, Women, and the State in the Post-Soviet Era*, won the Adele E. Clark Book Award, offered by ReproNetwork for groundbreaking and influential research, and received an Honorable Mention in the Association for Feminist Anthropology's Michelle Z. Rosaldo First Book Prize.

www.ingramcontent.com/pod-product-compliance
Lightning Source LLC
Chambersburg PA
CBHW020029040426
42333CB00039B/592